the
splendid
things
we
planned

the
splendid
things
we
planned

a family portrait

blake bailey

w. w. norton & company   new york · london

Author's Note
Most non-family names have been changed, for the sake of both privacy and clarity (for example, to avoid confusion when two different people have the same name). In some cases, a few identifying details have been changed as well.

Copyright © 2014 by Blake Bailey

Excerpt from *Up in the Old Hotel* by Joseph Mitchell, copyright © 1992 by Joseph Mitchell. Used by permission of Pantheon Books, a division of Random House, Inc.

"Yesterday When I Was Young" ("Hier Encore"). English Lyric by Herbert Kretzmer. Original French Text and Music by Charles Aznavour, © Copyright 1965 (Renewed) 1966 (Renewed) Editions Musicales Charles Aznavour, Paris, France. TRO – Hampshire House Publishing Corp., New York, New York controls all publication rights for the U.S.A. and Canada. Used by permission.

Portrait of Bailey family by David G. Fitzgerald used courtesy of David McNeese. Photographs of Blake and Scott Bailey used courtesy of Marlies Bailey.

For information about permission to reproduce selections from this book, write to Permissions, W. W. Norton & Company, Inc., 500 Fifth Avenue, New York, NY 10110

For information about special discounts for bulk purchases, please contact W. W. Norton Special Sales at specialsales@wwnorton.com or 800-233-4830

Manufacturing by Courier Westford
Book design by Chris Welch
Production manager: Julia Druskin

Library of Congress Cataloging-in-Publication Data

Bailey, Blake, 1963–
The splendid things we planned : a family portrait / Blake Bailey. — First Edition.
    pages cm
  ISBN 978-0-393-23957-7 (hardcover)
1. Bailey, Blake, 1963––Childhood and youth. 2. Bailey, Blake, 1963––
Family. 3. Bailey family. 4. Authors, American—Biography.
5. Biographers—United States—Biography. I. Title.
PS3602.A526Z46 2014
814'.6—dc23
[B]

2013039720

W. W. Norton & Company, Inc.
500 Fifth Avenue, New York, N.Y. 10110
www.wwnorton.com

W. W. Norton & Company Ltd.
Castle House, 75/76 Wells Street, London W1T 3QT

1 2 3 4 5 6 7 8 9 0

To Marlies and Scott

That's one of the damnedest things I ever found out about human emotions and how treacherous they can be—the fact that you can hate a place with all your heart and soul and still be homesick for it. Not to speak of the fact that you can hate a person with all your heart and soul and still long for that person.

—Joseph Mitchell, *Joe Gould's Secret*

the
splendid
things
we
planned

prologue

My brother Scott was born in 1960 and screamed a lot as a baby, until one night my parents left him in their dorm room at NYU and proceeded to the roof, where a locked door prevented them from splattering themselves on a MacDougal Street sidewalk. In later years they'd tell the story for laughs, but I wonder if they saw the humor at the time. In the "funny" version I always heard, there was no locked door, and they carried Scott to the roof with them; the question was whether to throw him or themselves off. For a while they stood there, staring down at the lights of Washington Square while my brother yowled and yowled as if to egg them on to their doom. Not wishing to inflict this racket on the populace, perhaps, they retreated downstairs with the burden still in tow.

Life had been a heady affair up to then. My father, Burck, had come to Manhattan as a Root-Tilden Scholar at NYU Law, on his way to fulfilling his promise as the most gifted young man in Vinita, Oklahoma, a gray blur off the Turnpike between Tulsa and Joplin. He was whip smart, top of his class, American Legion "Citizen of the Year," even something of an athlete; he insisted on playing football even though—at five-ten, 135 pounds—he wasn't really big enough and kept getting banged up, almost losing a leg to gangrene when it was stepped on by a steel cleat. My mother, Marlies, was an offbeat German girl who bore a striking resemblance to Shirley MacLaine. She'd come to the States a couple of years before, age nineteen, and took an apartment at the Hotel Albert with two Jewish girls who thought she was a kick and vice versa. She and my father had met on a blind date. Both were escaping a home life they found oppressive, unworthy of the personages they hoped to become. Then my mother got pregnant.

My father supplemented his scholarship by working at a liquor store, while my mother had to stay home with the baby. Home was a tiny room with a Murphy bed, on which my mother sat in a funk all day, hour after hour, while little Scott emitted one heart-shriveling shriek after another. He rarely slept. Sometimes his eyes would glaze as he screamed; he'd stare at some vague speck on the ceiling, as if screaming helped him concentrate on some larger plan. For her part (I imagine) my mother dwelled ruefully on the recent but dead past. She'd been having such a good time in America. Before marrying my father—before *this*—she worked in the gourmet shop at Altman's and got plenty of dates; her English was excellent, she was wistfully intellectual, and she liked to argue in favor of atheism and Ayn Rand.

The doctor had given her some sleeping drops for the baby,

which she ended up taking instead. Meanwhile she'd gone a little mad with postpartum depression. She couldn't keep food down, and had pretty much given up on eating. "I had huge milk-filled breasts and the waist of a ten-year-old," she remembered, wondering whether her milk had been somehow tainted by the dreariness of it all. Plus her crotch itched something fierce; the doctor had sloppily shaved her prior to slitting her perineum.

Many years later my mother and I had a lot of tipsy conversations about all this. *Where did we go wrong?* conversations. One night she started sobbing—drunk or not, she cried only in moments of the most terrible grief—and said she'd once done a terrible thing when Scott was a baby. This was around the time my father had almost died from a bleeding ulcer. As usual he'd been studying in the bathroom late at night, sitting on the toilet with tissue in his ears, when my mother heard a *thunk* (his head hitting the sink) and found him passed out in a fetal slump. While he was away at St. Vincent's, Scott redoubled his efforts to nudge our mother into the abyss—screaming and screaming and *screaming* as if to berate her for some ineffable crime against humanity. Marlies, in turn, tried frantically to calm him: nursed him with her aching breasts, changed and rechanged his diaper, shushed and cuddled and pleaded with him. Finally, beyond despair, she muffled him with a pillow. If the baby had struggled, writhed a bit, she might have forgotten herself and held the pillow in place a moment too long—but he only lay there as if to emphasize his helplessness. Even then, Scott had a knack for self-preservation in spite of everything.

When I later mentioned the episode, Marlies vehemently denied it. She's denied it ever since. So maybe she was only dreaming out loud that night, unburdening herself of a persistent but intolerable thought.

part I

day thief

A crucial difference between my brother and me was that he spoke German and I didn't—which is to say, he inherited my mother's facility and I inherited my father's all but total lack thereof; in fact, it became another aspect of Scott's curious bond with my mother, as they'd lapse into German whenever they wished to speak or yell privately while in my presence. Scott learned the language at age thirteen, during a solo trip to Germany to visit our grandparents, and on return he contrived to insult me in a way that would call attention to this superiority. I was ten and didn't brush my teeth as often as I might, so he dubbed me Zwiebel Mund, or "onion mouth." It stuck: he never again called me anything else unless he was angry or discussing me with some third party.

Mind, there were many variations. Usually he called me Zwieb, and what had begun as an insult assumed, over the years, the caress of endearment. In its adjectival form—Zwiebish, Zwiebian, etc.—it meant something like: pompous but in a kind of lovable, self-conscious way (as *he* saw it), or benignly self-absorbed (ditto) and given to odd, whimsical pronouncements because of this. The nuances were elusive and mostly lost on the world beyond my brother and me. There were also ribald noun variations—Zwiebel-thang, Zwiebonius, etc.—or, when he was particularly delighted (high-pitched) or admonishing (low), he'd throw his head back and say *Zwiiieeeeeeeeb!* with a faint, nasal Okie twang to the vowel sound. My brother had more of an accent than I, especially as we got older, due in part to the different company we kept and perhaps because he was often stoned. Kind people tell me I have little or no trace of an Oklahoma accent. If so, I have my mother to thank—her own English sounds, if anything, vaguely British—though my father too has mostly purged his deep, lawyerly voice of its Vinita origin, except when he's trying to connect with the common folk, and in any case he still pronounces the *a* in pasta like the *a* in hat.

And what, in turn, did I call Scott? I called him a very matter-of-fact (or deploring) *Scott*. No endearments on my end.

AFTER NYU, MY father was hired by Morrison, Hecker, Cozad & Morrison in Kansas City, where he and my mother and Scott lived in an apartment complex called the Village Green. I picture their two-story row house as a rather drab, dispiriting place, but of course it was paradise next to Hayden Hall at NYU. Life got steadily better. Burck's colleagues at the firm were a festive, hard-drinking bunch who thought Marlies was a hoot (she danced on tables at parties), and meanwhile she'd found "some kindred women" through volunteer work at the Nelson Art Gallery. One of her better friends was a gorgeous trophy wife who used to complain bitterly about things, and finally hanged herself in the attic.

The Village Green was aptly named, as its long blocks of housing units surrounded a big lawn perfect for frolicking toddlers. Scott played mostly with toy cars, pushing them back and forth in the grass while making a monotonous *vroom vroom* sort of noise; when the neighbor kids tried to join him, he'd gather up his stuff and leave. Indeed, he preferred the company of an imaginary friend named Ralphie. No doubt Ralphie was a quiet, thoughtful little chap like Scott, and hence a reasonable alternative to the real-life playmates at hand, so raucous and silly in comparison. The two-year-old Scott also had a great fondness for climbing, another maverick tendency: on the children's playground at the zoo was an old fire engine, and he'd scare my mother by skittering to the top while the other kids watched wide-eyed from below.

That was the year they decided to move back to Burck's home state. As Marlies would always tell it, they'd been driving through a blizzard to Vinita for the holidays, almost wiping out at one point when the car went into a spin. Then, at the Oklahoma border—like entering Oz—the snow stopped: not a flake in sight. "This is where I want to live," my mother announced. As luck would have it, the state's new attorney general was a friend of Burck's cousin, Bill Bailey, who urged my father to apply for assistant AG: the pay wasn't much, but it was a good way to build trial experience. Burck was hired a few weeks later, and in January 1963 they moved to Oklahoma City with me in utero.

AT THE BACK of my grandmother's house in Vinita was an ugly paneled room that used to be a screened porch. My grandfather had once gone there to drink in peace; Scott and I slept there during our childhood visits. One wall was covered with photographs of then-living relatives I knew slightly or not at all—for example, my great-uncle Tom and his wife, Louise: not only did these two refuse to smile for the camera, they appeared to make a positive effort to look nasty. Perhaps they thought it was more dignified. A few years later, when I was seventeen or so, I encountered my uncle Tom in the anteroom of the funeral parlor he ran with his (nicer) brother, Charles. This was maybe the second time our paths had crossed. Tom had a glass eye that stared obliquely over one's shoulder. After a brief chat he announced—apropos of nothing I can recall—that I was a bleeding-heart liberal just like my father. Tom's glass eye gave him a dreamy air as he sat there denouncing me.

The first time I ever heard the expression "not worth the powder it would take to blow them up" was when I asked my father about that photograph of Tom and Louise, whom I'd yet to meet at the time. In those days, as far as I could tell, my father divided his Vinita family into two basic categories: tiresome, bigoted creeps like Tom and Louise, and "salt of the earth" folk like my uncle Charles, who almost never left the environs of Craig County during his eighty-odd years on earth. The second kind of person was better than the first, of course, but I'm not sure either was particularly desirable.

My grandfather Frank was the local postmaster for twenty-five years. He'd served his country in both world wars, never missed a Rotary Club meeting, and (according to his obituary in the *Vinita Daily Journal*) could "cuss out his best bird dog then pet him as he would a child." A man's man, in short. When he first heard that his son had married a German, he was furious:

"I go over there to kill the bastards, and he marries one!"

Marlies was fretful, then, at the prospect of meeting this man for the first time (his remark had reached her somehow), and she asked her husband to suggest some of his favorite foods. But Burck was no help; his family, never mind their cuisine, had apparently made little impression on him, as if he'd grown up in a series of foster homes. So finally she chose something simple but tasty from the *Better Homes and Gardens* cookbook—corned beef, cabbage, and potatoes—and the man's heart was won. Or so she reductively tells it. The main thing, perhaps, was that Frank enjoyed having a comely young woman in his life, and a refreshingly eccentric one at that: far from scolding him for his drinking, she'd join him on the screened porch and match him snort for snort.

OKLAHOMA CITY WAS hardly a marvel of cosmopolitanism, though there were bits of wistful striving in that direction. My family moved to a neighborhood called the Village (no "Green"), whose street names—Manchester, Stratford, Sheffield, et al.— evoked the provincial charm of the Mother Country, as did a number of incongruous little motifs like wishing wells, Cotswold roofing, diamond-shaped casement windows, and the like. These seemed the remnant of some romantic, postwar builder, whom I imagine being shoved aside by moneymen who said, "Let's just get these fuckers *built*."

To my mother, even the bleakest species of Eisenhower-era, tract-house suburb—and the Village was that—meant comfort and efficiency *tout court*. It didn't faze her that they could only afford one car, for my father's use. When she'd go shopping at nearby Casady Square—a jolly promenade, the high point of her day—she'd fill my brother's stroller with grocery bags until only his stalwart little head stuck out. (Casady Square was a tableau out of Edward Hopper, its ugliness all the more stark in the dusty amber sunlight of Oklahoma: groceries, dry-cleaning, drugs, shoe repair—the bare necessities, as if life were a purely pragmatic interval between birth and eternity.) And her neighbors were so kind! The elderly couple next door gave her a ham on moving day; a minister invited her to join his church. Such decency, she decided, was at least somewhat indigenous to Oklahoma, and partly for that reason she never left.

EVERYTHING WAS BETTER by the time I came along. Marlies was resigned to motherhood, Burck was making a name for himself in the AG's office, and Scott seemed to want a little brother. We were a study in contrast. As a baby I rarely cried or fussed, which delighted my mother, who'd kiss the little button between my legs and watch me chortle and kick. But I think she actually preferred my brother: in my normalcy I was a bit insipid; Scott had a peculiar kind of gravitas. Indeed he seems conscious of that quality in all our photos from early childhood, as he stares at his drooling brother with a sort of wise passivity. His face in repose had become solemnly handsome.

My mother finally went back to Germany in 1966, when I was three years old, for her brother Richard's wedding; she took Scott along and left me in Vinita with Oma (whom we called "Oma from Vinita" to distinguish her from Marlies's mother, "Oma from Germany"). My father had work to do and stayed in Oklahoma City. He visited every other weekend or so, but it was a three-hour drive to Vinita. Scott and Marlies bonded, abidingly, during that trip abroad. They crossed on the *Nieuw Amsterdam*, and Marlies was laid low by a bad case of strep throat. As she would tell it and tell it over the years, Scott took care of her: he'd sit by her bunk and play with Ralphie or his bear or both, but as soon as she needed something he'd bolt to his feet and get it; other times he'd just watch her with large attentive eyes. My German grandparents were enchanted with him. There's a photo of the four standing on the gangplank, and Scott seems almost a parody of the well-behaved Little Man—dressed in a navy blazer and clip-on necktie, far too serious to smile; in another gangplank photo he clutches his Teddy as if it were an orphan he'd saved from drowning.

Meanwhile I was an unremitting misery to my grandmother in Vinita, and she emphatically told my mother as much. I'd thrown tantrums and broken some beloved tchotchkes. Evidently I didn't like being farmed out to Vinita, though of course I can't remember a thing about it.

I was aware that my parents found Scott more interesting, but it didn't bother me much. I took the long view, finding insidious ways to assert my own specialness. For one thing I affected to be a great reader and would bother my mother about ordering books from the catalogs we got at school; I loved the way these books smelled when I first cracked them open, but that was about it. My parents hinted, for my pains, that I was the smart one—or maybe that was just a sop they tossed me. My mother simply laughed when I brought *Dead Souls* home from the bookmobile in second grade. In general I was on the lookout for ways to capitalize on my brother's failings. If he wouldn't eat a certain food, say, I'd make a point of gorging myself on it. Also I'd use words that I knew would aggravate him: "Don't quarrel" . . . "I implore you" . . . "How uncouth."

For the most part, though, I liked my brother and he liked me. As we got older he'd let me play football with him and his friends, a privilege for which I was willing to take any amount of punishment. I cherished their good opinion. "Bronko Nagurski" my brother called me, after the legendary fullback: I'd butt heads with his bigger, helmeted friends and make them cry. I had a very hard head. The downside was that my brother took to proving how tough I was; for years he'd hide behind trees and hedges and hit me out of nowhere with bone-rattling tackles, and I'd just have to take it. I'd hear those last rapid footfalls just before impact—too late.

One day Scott and I were standing in front of the bathroom mirror when he stepped back, sighed, and said, "Don't you wish you were this handsome?" I considered him there in the mirror. "You *are* better-looking," I conceded. He was; there was no use denying it. My brother, happy that I knew it too, magnanimously claimed to be joking. I in turn was pleased with my own modesty, and something else: a sense that my brother wouldn't always be the golden boy. In his preening I detected a little protesting-too-much, an inkling that his luck was running out even then, at least in comparison with his hard-headed brother.

ONE TURNING POINT was a trip to Germany we took as a family in 1972, when I was nine and my brother twelve. My father chose me to accompany him to Stuttgart, where he wanted to visit his old army base and other haunts. (While at Westminster College in Missouri he'd run out of money and had to enlist for two years.) Marlies, who didn't want to go to Stuttgart, had urged him to take Scott instead of me; she thought Burck and I were both bumblers and together we'd be doubly so. Scott had been the responsible one ever since that precocious sojourn on the *Nieuw Amsterdam*, and the idea was that my monoglot father would get in some kind of trouble if he traveled without Scott's assistance. Burck was still in his thirties then, already a top antitrust lawyer in Oklahoma, a formidable man, and thus he decided to take me and to hell with my mother's advice.

On the train he taught me how to play chess, and later that night our taxi took us to a sinister neighborhood and dropped us at a hotel that turned out to be closed. My father stood pondering the Gothic letters on the locked door—"*Geschlossen?* . . . Oh! Wait!"—but the cab was gone and we couldn't find another. Four or five trains came and went, my father pounding the door of each, shouting at the passengers inside, but *whoosh whoosh whoosh* . . . until finally he discovered the big metal button one had to push to make the doors spring open. At his army base the next day we were accosted by MPs—the flag was at half-mast, I remember, because Truman had died the day before—and escorted to the CO's office, where we were reproached for wandering onto the base without clearance. I sat there in my little woolen parka, my feet kicking above the floor, amazed that my father had gotten us in trouble. That night he put me to bed and went out on the town alone. I panicked: I'd had my first-ever cup of coffee with dinner, my heart was pounding, and I was all but certain I'd never see my father again—he'd get lost and disappear, board the wrong train to nowhere, and what would become of me? When he finally returned I burst into tears, and he sat on the bed and hugged me to his chest.

From that point on, I was closer to my father than Scott was, and no doubt about it; we were a comfort to each other, all the more so over time.

FOR A WHILE my brother seemed to work harder for my parents' attention. He'd conduct elaborate surveys on random topics—carry a clipboard to the grocery store and jot down, say, tar and nicotine levels of various cigarette brands, though he didn't smoke and was, if anything, proud of the fact that our mother wolfed her Salems all the way down to the filter.

There was also a dog food survey, though I don't think we had a dog at the time. A given survey would go on for months. When Scott pursued his researches in Vinita ("What kind of cigarette is that?" he'd inquire of some old lady. "Can I see the pack?"), my grandmother would sheepishly joke about it, which did nothing to dampen his weird enthusiasm.

He became extravagantly neat. My mother helped him turn his bedroom into a cool seventies "pad" (think Greg's attic retreat in *The Brady Bunch*), complete with beaded curtains around the bed and so forth. Scott was so pleased with the effect that he took to sleeping on the floor rather than mussing his beads and remaking the bed.

Objects were arranged around the room with a kind of cryptic symmetry, and if I happened to pick something up and put it down somewhere else he was liable to hit me. His record collection was carefully alphabetized, and I was forbidden to use his turntable because I sometimes forgot to clean his records (or I cleaned them "wrong") with the plush little tool he placed in plain view for that purpose. He was lavishly fond of a fat white hamster named Algernon, whose Habitrail palace was disassembled each week and scrubbed with Pine-Sol. Scott had human friends too (they also failed to clean his records properly), but he still spent a lot of time alone in his room, his "pad," communing with Algernon.

One night in the paneled room at Oma's house he confided that he lived in two separate dimensions. The present one I knew. In the other he had a different and far more appreciative family, and no little brother. He described the whole setup in detail. The main conceit was that this other family was more or less opposite to the one we shared: blond like him (my parents and I were dark-haired), inclined to take him along when they traveled (as opposed to ditching him in Vinita), wholly devoted to him, in fact.

He became a bit tearful as he told it, as a sense of what he was missing in the here and now came over him. I started crying a little too. Already I felt as though we were about to say good-bye to each other forever.

Around the age of thirteen he became more and more arrogant. I think it was John Lennon, one of his heroes, who inspired him to flash a two-fingered peace sign (sneering) in almost every photo from that era, and "middle-class" was his favorite epithet—meaning the dull herd, etc.—an anathema he applied to the whole doltish world. His smile was an occasional simper of amused superiority. He was right about everything even when he wasn't. Once he corrected my use of the word "haberdasher"—he said it was a place to buy hats. I replied that one could get more than hats at a haberdasher, and the dictionary seemed to bear me out on that. My brother called the dictionary "a piece of shit" (his language was foul and getting fouler, another aspect of his rebellious persona), then slunk off to his room and slammed the door. One day he grabbed me by my shirtfront and yanked me into a punch that left half my face bruised and swollen. He'd always pushed me around a lot and blindsided me with those tackles out of nowhere, but this was different, and Burck was furious. Though he rarely spanked us, he gave my brother a smart lash with his belt, then let me decide whether Scott should get more of the same. I shook my head, but I had to think about it first.

Even as a boy I knew Scott's arrogance was pathetic, and in a secret way I was the more arrogant one, because I really believed in my essential superiority (at least where Scott was concerned). And lest there be any doubt, my father had pretty much told me so, though I wonder if that's what he intended at the time. During our frequent chess games I'd mention all the vicious things Scott had said about me and done to me, until one night my father remarked, "He's just jealous," and went on to say some nice things about my intellect and the like. Again, this was probably just a sop, though I was glad to have it. I could hardly wait to throw it in my brother's face.

I didn't wait long.

The year before, we'd moved to the country near the town of Edmond, about a half-hour drive via the expressway from downtown Oklahoma City. Burck had received his first six-figure fee after he'd successfully prosecuted an asphalt price-fixing cabal in a widely publicized trial. (Noting that my young father had opposed a team of wily, more experienced lawyers, the *Daily Oklahoman* called it a "David and Goliath" story: "But in the end people might have wondered: Who was David and who was Goliath?") Because of her lifelong love of Karl May, the fanciful German chronicler of the American West (Old Shatterhand et al.), Marlies had wanted a place in the country where she could keep Arabian horses and immerse herself in animal husbandry and whatnot. Thus my father bought eight acres of land in one of several rustic subdivisions north of the city, Deer Creek Estates, and built one of those blocky "modern" monstrosities that were all the rage in the seventies but still pretty daring in Deer Creek: a white-brick two-story with chocolate-colored trim, three balconies, a high slanted roof on one end, and a lot of shag carpeting and Peter Max wallpaper on the inside. My parents were enormously proud of the place, and why not? Just over a decade had passed since Hayden Hall.

One night my brother was babysitting at one of our neighbors' houses (some residual legend of responsibility clung to him), and I was home alone. I was ten years old, and I guess my parents thought I could handle the odd evening by myself. They were mistaken. A sudden sense of rural isolation had spooked me. In tears,

I called my brother and begged him to come home right away. Somehow or other he managed it—he got our neighbors on the phone at some dinner party and made up a bogus emergency so he could leave early—and when he came in the door I threw myself at him, kissing him on the lips. For a few minutes we loved each other better than anyone.

Our happy reunion didn't last. Ever since we'd come back from Germany the year before, I'd been fanatically attached to seven cartoon figures called Mainzelmännchen—little men from Mainz, whose fifteen-second antics were interspersed with commercials on German television. I had little rubber Mainzelmännchen that I played with constantly, most memorably in the rain, when the irrigated pasture on the property behind our house became an enchanted city of canals. For a while my brother was interested too, but less so over time—he was thirteen, after all. Unfortunately, the night he came home early from his babysitting job to comfort me was also the night he let me know once and for all that he didn't want to play with the Mainzelmännchen anymore, that he was *sick* of the Mainzelmännchen.

In deadpan earnest I told him I hated him. For a moment he looked stunned; then he began to cry. "You were so happy to see me," he sobbed, "and now you s-say you *hate* me . . ." It was a fascinating business—my brother crying over a trifle, so it seemed to me—and I didn't want it to end. So I told him, too, what our father had said while we were playing chess: "He says you're mean to me because you're jealous. Because I'm smarter than you and can do things like play chess and play the piano."

Rather abruptly Scott stopped crying; he nodded slightly, once, twice, as if this were something he'd suspected all along and now saw clearly, the way a person finally accepts the irrefutable fact of cancer. Without a word he went to his room and shut the door.

After an hour or so, a guilty panic got the better of me and I looked in on him. He was lying on the floor in that sleeping bag he used so he wouldn't muss the bed. In the dark I saw the glimmer of his staring eyes. "He didn't really say that," I ventured, but Scott didn't bother to dignify this with a response.

AFTER THAT NIGHT my brother made less of an effort to cultivate my parents' favor. He was particularly defiant toward Marlies, who was going through a Madame Bovary phase and seemed annoyed by the finer points of motherhood. Life in the country had been nice for the first year or so, but the rest of us didn't share her enthusiasms and she became bored and a little bitter. She took to spending long hours at the Old Dodge, a mall bar in Edmond, and was often tipsy when she came home to make dinner. At the best of times she was quick to slap or yell at us; volatile by nature, she'd been brought up in a German household so strict she'd put an ocean between it and herself. One night Scott made a typically snide remark at the dinner table, and just as typically my mother slapped him. I doubt Burck and I even looked up from our plates. But then my brother began shouting: "Don't you hit me! This is my house too and I can say whatever I want!" So my mother hit him again.

Suddenly they were both on their feet, scuffling along the kitchen floor. Marlies was still bigger than Scott and had the better of it, but he refused to give in. "You shut your mouth!" she yelled, her thorny gardener's hands flapping at his face, which was flushed with unrepentant rage. "I'm *not* going to shut up! I can say what I want! Don't you hit me anymore!" She pummeled him out of the kitchen and their voices trailed off down the hall, down the stairs, punctuated at last by a banging door. "And you *stay* in there, buster!" my mother bellowed. My father and I sat there looking at each other.

NOW IN HER midthirties, Marlies began taking classes at the University of Oklahoma in nearby Norman. She'd yet to get a college-equivalent degree, and anyway it was something to do. Not only was she an excellent student (she got straight A's on her way to an eventual master's in anthropology), but something of a party girl too. Enamored of all things Arabian, she mostly hung out with Arabic exchange students, who embraced the Afros, bell-bottoms, and chest-hair jewelry of seventies America. Two young men I remember in particular, Khalid and Muhammad, as well as their older friend, Walid, who was roughly my mother's age. When I came home from school in the afternoon, I'd find them all lounging around our living room with my mother and a few of her girlfriends—Penny and Lenore and Phyllis, the last of whom fancied herself a belly dancer and torch singer. A pall of cigarette smoke hung near the ceiling while the ice tinkled in big glasses of Scotch. "Heyyy!" Walid would greet me with a drunken growl, and Khalid would give me a dopey grin; Muhammad, the moody one, would look away. It all seemed harmless enough. Sometimes my mother would ask me to play piano, and Phyllis would sing along with a lot of harrowing coloratura: *"Chlo-eeee! Chlo-eeee!"*

My father was a good sport about things and at one point agreed to throw a big catered party for the whole Arabic cultural exchange program. In one of the photographs from this occasion my father is wearing a keffiyeh and smiling gamely; my mother is decked out in a kaftan, her sleeves drooping as she hugs my father around the neck. Probably I was in bed by then—anyway, I don't remember the keffiyeh. What I do remember is the small gathering at dusk as the caterer was setting up. My father was still at his office in Oklahoma City. I'd snuck out of my room to lurk around the swimming pool, and I watched, undetected, as my mother took Muhammad by the hand and led him off behind the propane tank, where their silhouettes came together kissing in the twilight. Then, a bit later, I followed my brother and his friend Warren at a stealthy distance as they left our house along the gravel driveway. By then I was dreading the worst. Standing behind one of the brick pillars at our entrance gate, I peered into the dark and saw Scott and Warren pause around a flaring match, then walk away with two embers swinging at their sides.

My father came home around eight or so—his usual time—and asked me to keep him company while he changed for the party. Off the master bedroom was a balcony overlooking the pool, and we could hear Marlies's friends hooting and splashing around below. "What's wrong, son?" he asked, pausing in his underwear to look at me. I was crying. I couldn't help it. Probably I shrugged and bit my lip, shaking my head, but my father persisted.

"I saw Scott and Warren," I said finally, "*smoking.*"

He nodded with a grave, thin-lipped look. Like most little brothers I had a tendency to tattle, but this was nothing like that, and my father knew it. Nor did he find my grief melodramatic, as it certainly seems in retrospect—devoid, that is, of the weird subjective dread I think we both felt at the time.

"Have you told your mother?" he asked.

I shook my head.

A bit later that night, at my father's behest, my mother met me in the garage (why the garage, I wonder). She seemed put out; I had taken her away from the party.

"What is it?" she asked.

I told her.

"Oh for Christ's sake!" She gave me a look of elaborate disgust, throwing her head back and rolling her eyes. "He's fourteen years old! Kids that age take a little *puff* now and then!" Unwilling to waste another second on me, she left the garage with a whirl of her silken hem, barking "Go to bed!" over her shoulder. I thought I'd get even by telling my father about her little monkey business with Muhammad, but I never did.

DURING HIS MIDTEEN years Scott didn't worry so much about his status in the family because he didn't have to—he had plenty of distractions. He was more handsome than ever: his face was clear, his hair was still golden blond in the summer, he'd grown a few inches and had better muscle tone than I ever would. I look at photographs of us together, shirtless around the pool, and it's just pathetic. No wonder he didn't mind when I was elected president of the seventh grade. Now that I was in junior high, we attended classes in the same building of a small rural public school, and the day of my election it promptly got back to me (as intended) that Scott had sneered at one of my classmates, "You people *must* be desperate."

A lot of the older kids hated me because of Scott. Big scary hicks with baseball caps advertising chewing tobacco or cattle feed would corner me in the halls and ask me if I was Scott's brother. In response to my apologetic nod, they'd bend down and give me a piece of advice: *don't be like your brother, unless you want to get your ass kicked.* And yet I can't remember Scott getting into any fights. I think he was careful not to cross the line, or was just too loftily disdainful of the whole redneck crowd to bother mincing words with them. Scott's friends were stylish worldlings like himself, children of commuters who lived in the same sort of upscale subdivisions (Sorghum Mill, Rambling Wood). They didn't play sports or attend FFA meetings; they acted. During Scott's sophomore year, our last in the country, he appeared in a scene from *Barefoot in the Park* as part of a "montage" production of duet acting and dramatic monologues; the Jane Fonda part was taken by his girlfriend, Barbie Benedict, a blandly cheerful brunette. All I can remember about Scott's performance was the natural way he took off his necktie, as if he'd worn one all his life. My parents and I were impressed by little touches like that.

What I saw of my brother at home was somewhat in contrast to the dashing (if controversial) figure he struck at school. Perhaps it was jealousy to some extent, but I found him a pretty despicable character. He was constantly baiting my mother, who didn't hit him anymore because he was too big and it would only prolong the nastiness. Instead she stayed away more than ever, rarely home when I returned from school in the afternoon, and often a bit drunk if she showed up later. Scott did what he could to make my life miserable too, insofar as he bothered. He mocked me constantly, repeating my every word in a girlish whine. Any protest on my part, emotional or not, was met with the same shtick: Scott would bunch up his face and say "*Aye-lie-lie!*"—a bawling baby. Sometimes I did cry, which really brought out the sadist in him, especially if our friends were around. "*Aye-lie-lie! . . . Aye-lie-lie!*" he'd cry over and over, gamboling about, shoving me, getting in my face. He'd force me to the floor and make me smell his farts, and once he insisted I watch when he climbed to the roof and took a shit off the chimney. Afterward he scrambled down and confronted me.

"What'd it look like, Zwieb?" he said, a little out of breath.

"What do you mean?"

" '*Whaddyoo meeean?*' . . . I mean—you stupid little shit—what does my asshole look like when the stuff's coming out?"

I just stared at him. If I said anything he'd only mock me, and I'm not sure I really understood the question.

"Down," he said, pointing, which meant I had to lie supine while he farted in my face.

"No! Leave me alone!"

" 'No! No! Leave me alone! *Aye-lie-lie!*' I said get *down* . . ."

Naturally I struggled, but it was no use.

Oddly or not, the more abusive he became, the more I wanted his approval. If he told me to do something I'd do it, usually, and not just because I feared some kind of reprisal. He'd taken to jumping off our second-floor balcony into the pool, which required a forceful push of the legs lest one hit the sidewalk or the fake boulders skirting the water. One day he and his friend Kent were jumping again and again, both of them naked, the better to flaunt their big wagging dicks and fresh growth of pubic hair for my benefit. They hectored me to jump too, until I stood naked and trembling on the balcony rail, clutching the rain gutter as I measured the distance below. "Better cover your balls!" Kent yelled, to which my brother added, "Your *middle* one too!" No sooner had I jumped—just clearing the rocks—than my brother clambered all the way up to the roof and ran soaring into the deep end. So much for proving my mettle.

TO MAKE MY mother happy we moved back to the city in the summer of 1976. Nobody minded but me. Our new house was in the shabbier part of an upscale neighborhood, Nichols Hills, and I hated it: it was too small and ivy-smothered in a way that struck me as seedy; there was no pool. My father admitted in the car, as he took us to see the place for the first time, that he'd already bought it on impulse: a done deal. I thought he meant the big Tudor I'd picked out during an earlier house-hunting excursion, but no. I was dizzy with disappointment. As we parked in front of our new house and got out of the car, I said "Yuck!"—which struck my father from behind like a vicious little pebble: he'd made this move under duress, hastily accepting the first offer he got on our place in the country because his family was falling apart out there; his back stiffened, he paused, then walked on. It helped that my mother was ecstatic. "Mein *häuschen*!" she gushed, and wouldn't let anyone paint the bricks or trim the ivy, until we discovered that the vines were actually pushing the roof off.

I had nothing to do until school started. My brother had his learner's permit and was allowed to drive my mother's red Porsche 914, the kind with the motor in the middle for a low center of gravity, the better to take hairpin turns at top speed, as Scott did with or without a licensed adult. Meanwhile I got it in my head that a hamster would solve my unhappiness, rather the way Algernon had helped my brother before he got muscle tone and pubic hair. My mother reminded me that my last hamster, Amy, had died of neglect only two years before, and my brother was glad to elaborate on this.

"Her tiny paw was thrust into the cedar shavings for a last, piss-soaked food pellet," he reminisced, and imitated the way Amy had looked in her death agony: little bug eyes glazed, paw gnarled, her once-pouchy cheeks hollow.

But I was only eleven then, I pointed out.

"I was eleven when I had Algernon," Scott said triumphantly. He turned to our mother. "You know why he wants another hamster? So he can give *that* poor bastard a funeral too. Remember the cigar box he decorated for Amy . . . ?"

And so on. One day as we drove away from the mall, sans hamster, I began to sob over the injustice of it all. *"Aye-lie-lie!"* said Scott, leaning over the front seat to put his face in mine. *"Aye-lie-lie!"* So my mother turned the car around and bought me a hamster I named Perkins, whose running wheel squeaked all night, all night, until he turned up dead in the laundry hamper a few weeks later.

MY SELF-ESTEEM WAS buoyed somewhat by my mother's friends, who were mostly gay and thought I was cute—that is, precocious-cute as well as cute-cute. I laughed at their naughty jokes, or rather I laughed at their compulsive way of telling jokes, of being naughty, as if they had all the time in the world and nothing much mattered anyway. One of my favorites, Uncle Ronny, used to tell jokes that were almost dimwittedly silly, but I liked the relish with which he told them. I can only remember one, but it's representative.

"... 'Can you spell the *van* in vanilla?' " he said, working up to the punch line of a long story about a customer in an ice cream parlor who couldn't seem to accept that they were out of a certain flavor. " 'Can you spell the *fuck* in strawberry?' And the guy says, 'There's no fuck in strawberry!' 'Well, that's what I've been trying to tell you for the past five minutes!' "

Actually I preferred Ronny's boyfriend, Uncle Paul, whose wit was more subtle and whose company was an easier, quieter business. Paul liked me too, and was perhaps the first adult (apart from my parents) who gave me reason to think I was special, or at least different in a promising way. As a little boy I liked to dance frantically to the last movement of Beethoven's Ninth (*feuertrunken*—"drunk with fire"—indeed), and that was a good thing, according to Paul, who also praised the simple but astute caricatures I liked

to draw. He himself was the younger brother of a famous art-
ist, and to this day I think Paul was almost as talented. Mostly,
though, he was content to dabble. He went through a phase of
making a campier brand of Joseph Cornell box, and one of these
he gave to my mother: exquisitely arranged were a little ivory bust
of Beethoven, a plastic pig, a five-pfennig piece, and a fortune-
cookie slip on which he'd inked the following legend: "Beethoven
pfucked a pig for pfive pfennig."

    We were natural pals, and growing up I liked nothing better
than spending time at his and Ronny's trailer in the parking lot of
a restaurant, Christopher's, owned by Ronny's white-haired, irascible dad. (Ronny had once married and sired a son—also gay—
so perhaps his father couldn't understand why the hell Ronny
had plumped for this kind of life instead of that; on the other
hand Ronny was a maître d' par excellence, and rich old ladies
would frequent Christopher's expressly to bask in the moonlight
of his flattery, so the arrangement was beneficial to both father
and son.) Paul and Ronny were the best babysitters a kid like me
could have. The restaurant was on the banks of a lovely pond,
and during the day we'd sit fishing on the dock, or go to a dumb
movie, or else they'd just let me run loose in the restaurant and
I'd crawl around the plush booths in the bar and play with that
fascinating soda gun with the lettered buttons on the back—this
in the crepuscular saloon light of noon, in the cool conditioned
air, while the soothing Muzak played and played. I was a kind of
mascot for that quirky place. One of Paul's many talents was cal-
ligraphy, and almost twenty years later—long after he'd broken
up with Ronny and gone to Los Angeles to work for his brother—
I went back to the soon-to-be-bulldozed restaurant and noticed
for the first time, framed on the wall, the original invitations for
the grand opening in 1968 (I was five), which declared in Paul's

florid hand: "Mr. and Mrs. BLAKE BAILEY request the honor of your presence . . ."

As for the Arabs, they mostly disappeared after we moved back to the city in 1976—all but Walid, and he was generally drunk and simply sat on the floor like a skinny, scowling Buddha, listing to and fro. One time he was sober enough to help me with my homework—he was pursuing a PhD at OU, his nominal reason for staying in the States—and my mother took a picture of us sitting there with the book cracked open on our laps. Another time I ignored or didn't see a sign (STAY OUT) taped to the door of my father's study, through which I had to pass to take my morning shower. Inside, Walid and my mother's friend Lenore were locked in a stiff coital embrace on the foldout couch, both hiding their faces as if that would render them invisible.

My mother had always cultivated gay men, but now that we lived in the city again they came to our house in force. The more lurid aspects of these daytime gatherings were concealed from me. I later found a cache of old photos that showed, say, Walid using our fireplace stoker to divert the fumes of amyl nitrate ("poppers") spilled on Lenore's shirtfront. I saw none of that. To my mother's credit, the drugs were stashed and the zippers zipped in time for my return from school, and everyone would leave for the Free Spirit disco a few hours later, after a cordial drink with my father, home at last from work and wanting only to eat dinner and go to bed.

Everyone who floated into the orbit of the local demimonde came to our house at one time or another—the actor Van Johnson, for example, who'd been a big MGM star in the forties and fifties and now was in town for a dinner-theater production of *Send Me No Flowers*. At the time I hadn't seen any of his movies, but when I finally got around to it I was impressed: costarring in *The Caine Mutiny* with Humphrey Bogart, no less, the man gave a credible performance as a rugged but sensitive naval officer. Almost a quarter century after that movie, he padded out of a rented limo in our driveway, wearing some sort of eye makeup and calling my mother "Ruth Roman." I was charmed, though he clearly preferred my brother, then at the peak of his adolescent beauty. When the celebrated actor took leave of Scott with a hug, he slipped a plump, liver-spotted hand into Scott's pants and copped a feel. Scott expressed some token protest as the limo pulled away, though he was plainly rather pleased with himself. "I felt honored," he admitted to my mother afterward.

AS LUCK WOULD have it, our new house was a block away from a parochial school attended by one of my best friends from the country, Brian, whose parents were devout Catholics and didn't mind the long drive into the city each day. My own parents, debonair atheists both, liked the fact that the school was only a block away. Toward the end of the summer I took the eighth-grade entrance exam while my brother made a point of walking back and forth past the open classroom door with his arms extended like the crucified Christ.

Scott also got a Catholic education at Bishop McGuinness High School, where he soon had a girlfriend named Sally, who struck me as stupid but nice. Because she couldn't keep her hands off my brother, he liked to find pretexts for bringing her into my room like a prize monkey. I had narrow beds arranged in an L-shape with an eight-track stereo built into the corner table, and those two would wrestle around to the music while I sat chastely abashed on the other bed. In fact I felt sorry for the girl: she gazed at my brother with a kind of vacant adoration that, I could tell, was already grating on his nerves; also her father was a third-rate shyster named Wayne who liked to be called Dr. Wayne because of his Juris Doctor. Sally's fate was sealed by my father's gleeful teasing: "Son," he'd say to my brother, "I have this bad pain in my asshole. Next time you see *Dr.* Wayne, could you ask him to have a look?"

I envied such dilemmas as a vulgar, stupid girlfriend who put out. I was unpopular at my new school and very depressed about it. I'd done everything wrong. At my other school I'd been the kind of audacious wit whom other seventh-grade boys tend to emulate and elect class president; eager to reestablish myself as such, I regaled my new homeroom with what I thought was a spot-on imitation of Linda Blair in *The Exorcist*. Nobody laughed; nobody had seen *The Exorcist*. My teacher was so embarrassed for me that he chose to ignore this sudden eruption of guttural profanity. Perhaps he thought I was nuts. In a flustered way he cast about for a change of subject and didn't look at me the rest of the period. My next class was Spanish, where we were given a diagnostic quiz to determine how much of the language we'd retained over the summer. I'd retained nothing, since I hadn't taken Spanish in seventh grade like the rest of my classmates; nevertheless, I gamely copied a few sentences from my neighbor's paper. I hadn't gotten far when our teacher, Miss Hernandez, asked if I was cheating.

"No!"

The woman snapped up my quiz. "Yo soy Mateo," she read aloud (this appeared under the prompt "Tell us about yourself in Spanish"), and everybody laughed, including Miss Hernandez and Matt, the guy sitting next to me.

I sat alone in the cafeteria that day. My old friend Brian, who was in a different homeroom, already knew of my disgrace and was pointedly avoiding me. I was aware of people murmuring around me, about me, and I could hardly swallow my food. Finally we adjourned to the playground. I was thinking I'd ask a teacher for permission to go to the bathroom, where I could hide in the stalls until the bell rang, when somebody called my name. It was Brian, surrounded by his smiling, waving friends. Elated, I trotted over.

"See the top of the monkey bars?" said Mark Roach, the funniest kid in school. He pointed at the knobby apex and I nodded. "The first person to touch that thing in the middle wins. Ready? . . . Go!"

We all clambered up. Galvanized by what I thought was some kind of redemptive crucible, I beat the others easily and slapped my hand on the knob. It came away sticky. The others were laughing as they jumped off the bars and ran away. They'd each taken turns hawking loogies on the top knob to see if I was really as lame as everyone said. I'd passed the test with flying colors.

For the rest of that first month or so, my only friend was a kid named Weldon, whose claim to fame was twofold: (a) he had the oldest parents in school, older than most of our grandparents, and (b) he liked to hit himself on his shaggy, oversized head with rocks whenever people happened to be looking. We both collected comic books. Later I teased him mercilessly by way of distancing myself once I'd gotten more suitable friends, and because I suspected that Weldon and I were a pair of sorts, and I didn't want to be a pair with Weldon. Not long ago I heard that Weldon had died, and my only surprise was that he'd made it all the way to forty-something.

IN HIGH SCHOOL Scott showed promise as an actor, and perhaps his greatest triumph was his portrayal of the Hare in *The Great Cross-Country Race*. Grown to his final height of six-two, Scott looked like a lanky, long-eared marionette as he bounced around the stage on his big prosthetic Hare feet, mocking the

Tortoise, who was played with a lot of comic lethargia by his best friend, Todd.

I went to the cast party, I can't remember why. Todd, who'd made such a lovable, folksy old Tortoise, lay on his back pouring vodka down his throat. Scott sat next to him on the floor, smoking, occasionally taking a swig from one of Todd's bottles. Suddenly Todd blew puke in the air like a surprising geyser, spattering himself head to foot with half-digested finger food. He went on puking like that for the rest of the night, though never so dramatically as those first bursts. After that night, I rarely saw Todd completely sober outside of school; his eyes had a kind of nonscratch surface, and his mouth always hung open with quiet puzzlement. Tousled hair and all, he reminded me of Hoffmann's *Struwwelpeter.*

For Scott's sixteenth birthday he'd inherited the Porsche 914 from Marlies (who now drove a royal blue Cadillac Coupe de Ville), and one night he was driving with his usual lunatic abandon when he hit a slick spot on a winding road near the golf course and smashed sideways into a tree. My father had the car fixed, at great expense, and insisted my brother get an after-school job to pay for basic maintenance and build his character. So, for the rest of his time in high school, Scott worked as a busboy at one of the better restaurants in town, where a gay friend of the family was chef. Meanwhile he continued to crack up the Porsche every so often, claiming all the while that he was a superlative driver, the victim of rotten luck.

LIFE WITH MY family was becoming a serious bummer for all concerned. Scott fought constantly with Marlies, who could hardly stand to be home without a cluster of buffering friends, though they too were beginning to pall. She compensated by spending more and more time in Norman, near the university, until finally my father bought her a one-bedroom condo there. For a while she was home maybe four times a week, then three, then for the odd weekend. By then I had a few more friends, and I stayed at their houses as often as possible.

My brother's comings and goings, more conspicuous when Marlies was around to wrangle with, became increasingly furtive. Mostly he holed up in his room with a friend or two, their conversation muted by booming music. If Burck knocked on the door—lightly at first, then pounding to be heard—the music would suddenly gulp out and Scott would appear with a look of alert, almost comic solicitude, wide-eyed and nodding, a performance so bizarre that my father began to go his own way too. He and I still played chess now and then, or ate a sad frozen meal together, talking about anything but family.

Once I snuck into Scott's room and glanced at his bankbook (he liked to leave this out in the open as a token of his independence): from a peak balance of a thousand dollars or so, his savings had wasted away in increments of thirty or forty a week, and now hovered around two hundred. This in spite of the fact that he never bought anything but records that I could see. Another time I picked up the phone in my room (Scott and I had a common "children's line") and overheard him talking to his friend Pat, whom everyone called "Paht" because of the affected way he pronounced his *a*'s and because he smoked a lot of pot.

"And then I stood up and it was like *whoa*—" Paht was saying. "I got the biggest rush, mahn, like you wouldn't believe . . ."

My heart was pounding when I put the phone down. I was still in eighth grade and didn't know what "rush" meant in the druggy sense, but I could imagine. Another time I walked home late from a friend's house and saw the light on in my brother's window, which fronted a fairly busy street in our genteel neighborhood. I leaned over a hedge and looked inside: Scott was sprawled naked on the bed, alone, staring through slitted eyes at the ceiling, slowly plucking at his pubic hair.

That year was the first and last time we were photographed as a family for our Christmas card, something my parents had always considered bourgeois. Perhaps they thought if we perpetuated an illusion of domestic serenity it would come true to some extent. Perhaps, too, there was a kind of curatorial impulse to preserve our little unit for posterity before the final wave broke and dispersed us. The photographer posed us under a tree in our backyard. I remember poring over the contact sheets a week or so later and finding something wrong with almost every shot: our two Saint Bernards, Gretchen and Bruno, kept lurching to their feet and turning their heads the wrong way; Scott couldn't help but look moody and unpleasant, while I looked like a grinning idiot. Happily, a single photo was all but perfect: my parents were both beaming—aging well in spite of everything—the dogs were just so, Scott looked handsome and sane, and I looked as though I were caught in the midst of an orgasm, such was my almost frantic attempt to seem happy. The dogs too were smiling gamely, though Bruno was already suffering from the heart disease that would kill him within a month or so, and Gretchen followed close behind, and we didn't have any more dogs after that.

ONE DAY THAT spring I was sitting in my room with a few friends when I heard—when everybody heard—my mother weeping with perfect abandon in the adjacent master bedroom. We stopped whatever we were doing (some sort of board game) and looked at each other. I can imagine my thoughts at that moment: first, I made a mental note never to have friends at my house en masse again, and then it occurred to me, as I looked at their stunned and staring faces, that everyone but me came from a conventional middle-class home where the worst disasters were kept under wraps, and finally I decided I'd better go see what the deal was. I asked my friends to let themselves out, and they were happy to oblige.

Marlies was prostrate on the bed, though I noticed with annoyance that she kept her head averted so that her awful noises were unmuffled by the pillow. I'd seen her cry maybe five times before, but never like this. Something terrible had happened, all right. I sat beside her, patting her back, and warily asked what was the matter. Amid harrowing glottal sobs she told me:

"Scott's on d-*drugs* . . . long time now . . . everything . . ."

"Who told you this?" I asked.

"Everybody knows. Everybody at the GBR"—Grand Boulevard Restaurant, where Scott was a busboy—"t-talks about it . . . I don't know what to *do*. He doesn't listen to—to . . . I can't tell P-papa . . ."

Scott appeared in the doorway. He looked apprehensive in a vaguely amused way, as though he knew what was happening and found it absurd like everything else.

"What's going on?"

"She says you're taking *drugs*." I tried to make my voice sound a little weepy too, but it didn't come off. With a resigned smirk, my brother took my place on the bed and made to comfort my mother. For a minute or so I stood glowering at him, but I got the impression they wanted to be alone.

MY BROTHER CONCEDED his pot smoking but said that the other rumors (PCP, THC, various pills and powders) were fucking lies. He also made it clear that pot was no big deal and he had no intention of quitting. In fact he became a lot less furtive after that. He openly subscribed to *High Times* and kept elaborate paraphernalia in his room; I remember a two-foot bong called "the Skydiver" that involved pulling a ripcord to uncork the stop and release a massive hit of smoke. There was always a fresh "lid" of pot in the top right-hand drawer of his desk, along with cigarette papers and a nifty rolling device that produced joints as taut as Marlboros. All this was probably to the good—he didn't have to pretend anymore in that creepy wide-eyed way of his—but he also insisted on talking about it. On the rare occasions that the four of us still had dinner together, my brother would proselytize about how cool it was to watch this or that movie, or listen to this or that record, while stoned. Marlies tended to be mildly deploring in a this-too-shall-pass sort of way, but Burck's lips would thin and he'd chew his food with a kind of haggard bitterness.

Now that my friends and I were freshmen in high school, we'd decided to smoke marijuana too, or at least try it. I didn't tell Scott: now that he was a known stoner with a couple of car wrecks under his belt, I was indisputably the Good Son and wanted to keep it that way. The problem was getting the stuff. The three or four big dealers in school were all friends of my brother, and the whole crowd spent every spare moment on the "smoking porch" talking about getting high. Finally we bought a few joints for fifty cents apiece from one of the more peripheral friends, who called the stuff "killer Okie weed" and tried to entice us to buy a whole lid for ten dollars. We smoked the joints during halftime of a high school football game, sitting on the grass behind an unmanned concession stand.

The next morning my brother stood in the bathroom door with a gloomy, browbeating look.

"Don't you start getting into this," he said.

"What're you talking about?"

"You know."

So the pot dealer had told my brother. I went back to brushing my teeth, while my brother stood there watching me.

"I wouldn't worry about it," I said, and spat. "I didn't even get off. I have no idea what the big deal is."

This was true. And who was my brother to say no? Who indeed. A few days later—perhaps that same day—he reversed himself, insisting that I make an "informed decision" about smoking pot.

"I already have," I said. "I don't want to do it anymore."

"Just a few more times."

"No, thanks."

The following Monday, Scott pulled his Porsche into a little park on our way to school and began loading his bong. He made the thing hiss and gurgle and then passed it over. I took a hit and coughed explosively, soaking my lap with bong water. The stains didn't show on my navy corduroys, but all the potheads at school observed that I "reeked," while my sexy English teacher gave me a look of knowing admonishment. And I wasn't even stoned.

THAT FALL MY brother and I were in the high school play, *Death Takes a Holiday*. Scott had the lead as the dashing, vaguely foreign Prince Sirki (a.k.a. Death), and I was the sybaritic old Baron who engages the Prince in philosophical colloquies about a Life Well Spent. A few years back I'd been enrolled in the Children's Theater Workshop at Oklahoma City University, and was deemed good enough to be picked out of a class of fifteen or so to play the juvenile role in a college production of *Ah, Wilderness!*

Scott was contemptuous: "Acting is more than just memorizing lines," he sneered, when he caught me practicing in front of a mirror. He thought I was copying him again. Around that time he'd been reading a lot of Salinger and hence wrote a short story about an impossibly precocious toddler who kills himself because the adult world is a terrible place. Inspired by his example, I began a story titled "Don't Go into the Basement" about a monster in a basement. I was in the home stretch—the heroine was descending the steps, rather foolishly under the circumstances—when my brother, peeking over my shoulder, began reading aloud with leering disdain. Neither of our fiction-writing careers progressed much further.

But we made a good team as actors, or rather we enjoyed working together. My brother was one of the few seniors in the cast of *Death Takes a Holiday*, and he comported himself like Brando on the set of *The Godfather*—like a zany paterfamilias, mooning the other actors, obscenely improvising, cutting up a lot in general. Of course he was stoned most of the time. Our drama teacher was a clueless woman who wanted to be called by her first name; she was fired after that first year on the job. I can't remember her ever reproaching my brother.

Scott seemed to think his talent had outgrown our provincial high school, or at least this particular production. The day before dress rehearsal he asked me to run lines with him, whereupon the worst was revealed: he could only recite odds and ends that he'd soaked up through repetition, and there were quite a few longer speeches that he hadn't even begun to memorize. I was appalled; I was going down with the same ship after all.

"What the hell have you been *doing* these past two months?" I said with sincere amazement.

His reaction was curious. Without a word or change of expression he yanked me to my feet and punched me in the chest as hard as he could. I managed to gasp some sort of protest, and he shoved me over a table in our living room and began kicking me there on the floor. Anything I said or did seemed to provoke him, so I stopped struggling and simply grunted with what I hoped was a kind of poignant agony. If anything, this had the opposite effect: when one of his kicks made my head crack against a doorjamb, I affected a semiconscious daze ("*Unnnh*") and my brother began taunting me. " '*Unnnh*'—! '*Unnnh*'—!" he mimicked, kicking. The size difference between us was greater than ever (I was maybe five-five, the victim of a late puberty), and so he went on kicking and hitting me from room to room, careful not to mark my face lest our parents find out how bad the beating was. Toward the end he began to accompany his blows with a histrionic monologue about how everyone was *against* him (kick), how no one would *help* him (kick), and so on. We ended up in our father's study. I cringed on the sofa while my brother stood over me ranting and waving his fist. Then he fell to his knees and threw his head in my lap. He was crying or pretending to cry. The idea was that *I* should feel sorry for *him*.

I didn't feel sorry for him. He'd just beaten the shit out of me because he felt like blowing off steam, and now he was pretending to be in the midst of a terrible strain—because nobody would *help* him. I resolved to bide my time until this crazy bastard was out of the house, to be careful above all, and to make him pay for this little episode somewhere down the road.

I told nobody. Too humiliating. On the opening night of the play I was joking around in the dressing room—I'd flung off my shirt and begun flexing my spindly chest—and a girl in the cast, for whose benefit I flexed, said "Oh my *God*" and covered her mouth. My chest was an ugly mass of bruises, as though I'd been trampled by something large and hoofed. I can't remember what excuse I made.

One benefit of my brother's cathartic outburst was that it sobered him into memorizing his lines somewhat. Every time he was about to speak onstage there was a fraught little pause, as though he were pondering the world and its sorrows, but I knew the truth. "Come come, your Highness!" I couldn't resist ad-libbing in my role as the bluff old Baron. "Life is short! Out with it!"

A WEEK OR so later, when it was clear I wasn't going to rat him out to our parents, my brother gave me a peace offering: several fluffy buds of high-grade marijuana, stuffed in one of those plastic 35-millimeter film containers. I'd noticed in my brother's bankbook a recent lavish withdrawal of eighty-five dollars (leaving the total balance in two figures), and I assumed this was part of that purchase. He'd handed it to me with some brusque remark as we drove to school one day. I didn't bother telling him I didn't want it, as he'd only become abusive and perhaps contrive to beat the shit out of me again. When I got home that afternoon I tossed the little canister into some bushes under my bedroom window, which made me feel virtuous, or anyway better than my brother.

I retrieved it the following weekend, when my friend Matt ("Yo soy Mateo") and I went to the French Market Mall to see *Saturday Night Fever*. That afternoon he'd ridden his bike to a head shop in a distant neighborhood, where he bought a pipe that appeared to be cobbled together from bits of cast-off plumbing. Matt proposed to smoke some ridiculous amount of dirt weed—neither of us had really gotten high yet, but Matt was enamored with the whole hobbyist side of pot smoking and determined to persevere—so I told him about the better stuff I'd tossed in the hedge. We smoked two fat buds of it in a field beyond the parking lot and then hurried to get in line for the movie. The mall's Vieux Carré facade seemed not only kitschy but surreal and faintly menacing; the shortest kid in our class, Phil Philbin, came up to us in line and said hello; for some reason I felt a sudden, immense pity for Phil and began patting his head. Then I was watching the movie and then the movie was over. I remembered exactly this much: Travolta's feet gliding along the sidewalk during the opening credits, his father hitting his hair at the dinner table, and Donna Pescow pulling a train in the car and crying about it afterward. I had no idea what Travolta was doing with that other, skinnier woman at the end of the movie, or why the movie had ended at all. Years later, when I watched it again, I was struck by how it all fit together.

From then on I never failed to get high when I smoked, no matter what the quality of the dope. That would have been fine, except I didn't much like being stoned and still don't; it was a phase that pretty much ended after my freshman year—to be exact, after a "Youth Group" session at the parish house in our neighborhood, where we'd gather once a week to play Ping-Pong and Foosball and the like, or so the alibi went. I spent one of these nights smoking a bong in Paht's car with a group of people I hardly knew. The whole scene depressed me: I knew Paht would brag to my brother about how wasted he'd gotten me, that he and the others would still be getting stoned and talking about it for many dreary, dreary years to come. But the worst part was when my father stopped in my room afterward to say good night; he smelled smoke in my hair and asked me about it. I mumbled something about how a lot of people smoked at these Youth Group things, that the place was just really smoky, and he seemed to accept this and went away. My heart was banging so hard the blanket trembled.

SCOTT'S LOOKS BEGAN to fade toward the end of high school. As he lost the last of his baby fat, his face became narrow and angular, and its rather strange shape was accentuated by the way he wore his hair, long and lank, parted precisely down the middle like the later John Lennon's. The main problem was acne. I used to have a photo of Scott from this time, thrusting his cheek toward the camera to show off his many pimples.

My face was still perfectly clear at age fourteen—that is, during Scott's last months in high school, when I became the better-looking one. I knew this because my mother's gay friends began to make a bigger fuss over me, and one of them actually told my brother (because he'd asked) that I was the "tastier" of the two. This made me smug, and I wasn't averse to playing the flirt, at least for a while. The fat chef at the GBR, for example, had an obvious crush on me; an amateur magician, he'd regale me with gadgety little tricks in his office that resulted in elaborate desserts that I was then welcome to eat. Another old friend of my mother, a tall guy with a comb-over named Roger, began to draw me out on the phone when my mother wasn't home to take his calls. With a kind of weary petulance he'd insist that his IQ was over 160, that I should listen to him and take him more seriously. Roger had a responsible job in public relations (at night he danced with a tambourine at the Free Spirit) and my parents trusted him once to house-sit while they were out of town, lest Scott trash the place in their absence. As it happened, Scott was elsewhere and I was left alone most of the time with Roger, who sat around the house in bikini underwear and one night offered me a Quaalude.

Marlies was in a ticklish position. Her own conduct was hardly beyond reproach, as she was still in the midst of a hedonistic phase (though this was on the wane), and moreover she felt somewhat justified in making up for lost time: growing up in a burgherish German home had been stifling, whereas her subsequent emancipation in Manhattan was rudely interrupted by pregnancy and marriage. "Do as I say, not as I do" was the unspoken mantra of her parenting style. She was a great believer in temperate habits for children, the idea being that one becomes jaded if given the chance to indulge too soon in pleasures of the flesh.

That said, Marlies was the opposite of a conscious hypocrite and refused to act shocked about things that didn't shock her. She was less and less shocked by my brother's vagaries, and less inclined to express whatever shock she felt. For his part Scott never hesitated to point out her own dissipation when she tried to remonstrate about his; it was the burden of their many squabbles. Also, my mother was trying hard to understand Scott, a long process of self-hypnosis that would ultimately turn her into his foremost apologist. At the time it made her less than objective. When, for example, we found him straddling the roof of our garage in the nude—he was, of course, stoned out of his gourd—Marlies good-naturedly tossed him a pair of pajama bottoms, which he proceeded to wrap around his pelvis like a loincloth. A photo of this episode appears in one of my mother's albums over the twinkly caption "My nutty first-born!"

One night we sat at the dinner table, the four of us, discussing Scott's plans for his senior prom. By then he was dating a girl named Kara, who was always smirking about something, a smirk that became vague and almost vanished into politeness (ironical) when she spoke to adults. I never heard her say anything clever, so I suppose she was just zonked most of the time, a sphinx without a secret.

Scott went over his prom agenda, smiling at the subtext of how wasted he'd be, and finally announced that he and Kara had reserved a hotel room for the night. My father's chewing slowed and he narrowed his eyes at my brother. It might have ended there, but my mother was in a provocative mood.

"What?" she said to my father. "You think he's a virgin at his age?"

My father's lips thinned.

"You think other kids won't be doing the same thing? That they're not having *sex* at that age?"

And so on, and *on.* I suppose she meant to model a liberal tolerance of Scott's lesser peccadilloes, or perhaps she felt piqued by my father's rectitude, by what she liked to think at such moments was his underlying provincialism. Mostly, though, I think they were just fed up, both of them, that each blamed the other for any number of things. I looked at Marlies's bright eyes as she baited Burck, looked at Scott's besotted little grin, and I alone seemed to know that Burck was about to blow. I asked to be excused. My father gave me a quick nod, a flick of his chin, eager to get rid of me.

I'd just closed the door to my room when I heard the crash. I rushed back to the kitchen and saw my father standing over my mother, her raised arms trembling slightly; otherwise neither moved nor spoke. My brother was on his feet. I fled.

THOUGH HIS GRADES had fallen those last two years of high school, my brother was accepted into the Tisch School of the Arts at NYU. He was going to study acting. He got excellent recommendations from some of his teachers.

His last summer at home was a blur of disaster. It was then that Scott totaled the Porsche for good—or maybe, since it was the fourth or fifth time he'd wrecked it, my father just stopped paying for repairs. Scott also managed to alienate all but his most worthless friends. One guy who was a year younger than he, a fellow actor named Kevin, looked up to Scott as a kind of mentor and filled three pages of Scott's yearbook with a touching tribute. My brother responded by writing "Dear Kevin" at the top of a blank page in Kevin's yearbook, at the bottom of which he wrote "Sincerely, Scott." I had no idea what it was all about and didn't ask when Scott showed me, proudly, what he'd done.

One night he was arrested with Kara and another couple; I can't remember the details except my brother had resisted the police in some way and been roughed up a bit. In the middle of the night my father went to get him out of jail. Marlies and I were sitting at the kitchen table, having a desultory talk about the awfulness of it all, when Scott preceded my father through the back sliding door. His long hair was wrapped in a bandanna and he was strutting on the balls of his feet in a cocky, defiant way, weaving a bit from the lingering effects of whatever drugs he'd taken. He had the beginning of a black eye.

"The Oklahoma City cops," he said. "The royal scam."

That last phrase was the title of a Steely Dan album he liked. By then his cultural references were all but entirely derived from the more pretentious rock bands. He no longer read Salinger or any other fiction.

"Oh Scott," my mother said wearily. "You're just disgusting."

We all sort of nodded. My brother sneered and went to his room. There was nothing much to say. We drifted back to bed.

I was half-asleep when I became aware of Scott standing in the doorway. The light was behind him, but I could make out his slitted eyes and curled lip.

"You've got them scammed," he was saying. "Only a matter of time . . ."

He was shaking his head in a dopey, wondering way. I asked him to leave. He folded his arms and slumped against the door frame.

"I know you," he went on. "I know what you're like. You're gonna be just like me. You're gonna be worse. Look at you, you little fuck . . ."

On and on. I kept telling him to get out, and finally I began to scream. My brother went on in a hissing monotone, electrified by the effect he was having.

"Scream for Mommy," he said. "Scream for Daddy . . ."

My room was connected to the master bedroom via a bathroom, at the door of which my father appeared in his robe. He flicked on the light and stood there. At that moment he looked like a washed-up pug rising for the last round on guts alone. His face was mournful, puzzled; perhaps he was wondering why he'd worked so hard for *this*—a houseful of drunken queers, Arabs, a hopped-up son . . . how did this *happen*?

"Get him out!" I was screaming, thrashing in my bed as though a rattlesnake were under the sheets. "Get him outta here!"

Burck silenced me with a wince, then walked across the room and took Scott gently by the elbow. He guided him down the hall and out of sight. Then I heard Scott's voice rise in protest, and I followed to where the two stood beside the back sliding door. My father was in the process of throwing Scott out of the house, and I grabbed a heavy poker from beside the fireplace. I was almost hoping Scott would make some move on our father—I was drawing a bead on that silly bandanna of his—but instead he stood pleading in a wheedling, infantile way.

"Remember when you first saw me onstage, Papa? And you thought maybe I *had* something? That maybe I wasn't all bad? Papa . . . ?"

He was crying or pretending to cry. Burck sighed; he looked small in his bathrobe, standing beside my lanky brother.

"I never said you were 'all bad,' son. I never thought it. But I'm *tired* now, and I want you to go." He flung open the sliding door and pointed into the darkness. "Out."

Out my brother went with a tragic stumble, muttering how he'd never expected to be treated this way by his own family.

AND THEN IT was August and Scott was packing a big steamer trunk for NYU. I remember feeling tolerant about things. Scott had just gotten a haircut and looked clean and fit, sober and somewhat chastened, eager to prove himself in the greater world. He made much of the fact that he was attending our father's alma mater, that they were on the same level more or less, and such was my hopefulness that I didn't bother to point out that our father had gone to NYU *Law* School on a famous scholarship because he'd worked hard and stayed out of trouble and even then he'd had to take a job in a liquor store and never, ever would it have occurred to him to pursue some half-assed boondoggle (all bills paid) such as *acting* as a so-called course of higher study. That's what I was thinking in the back of my mind, but I was also willing to believe that Scott's behavior these last few years had been a kind of purging, that the worst was over, that his worthless friends would find themselves banished like so many Falstaffs from that day forward. I kept Scott company while he packed, and watched with smiling complaisance as he made room at the bottom of his trunk for his various bongs and other paraphernalia. Finally I helped him lug the thing out to my father's car.

"Well, Zwieb—"

"Well—"

I wasn't going to the airport. Burck wanted to talk to Scott alone for that last half hour or so, and that was fine with me. I was eager to move my stuff into Scott's bigger, better-appointed room. I started to give him a brisk hug, a stiff whack on the back, but he held me there and stroked my head in a way that embarrassed me. "You behave yourself," he said in a thick whisper, and when he let go his eyes were red. He'd taken to affecting a flat, twill cap he'd bought at an army surplus store, and he put this on now with a little flourish of adjustment. It looked ridiculous, and sad, and my heart went out to him for the first time in years.

HE LASTED MAYBE two months at NYU. From the start his letters to my parents were long and weird and woefully confiding. He had much to say about his roommate, a fellow acting student named Oscar. Scott was convinced that Oscar wanted to fuck him and was therefore a "pathetic faggot." Eventually, though, the roommates seemed to reach an understanding. The only bit of Scott's NYU correspondence that I can remember with perfect clarity was something he wrote after a long disquisition on the nature of his all but hopeless alienation: "I mentioned this to Oscar, and he just looked at me and said 'Everybody's alone, Scott.' "

One night Burck and I sat in the kitchen talking. He kept losing the thread and peering into the ether, rubbing his chin. He'd puff out his cheeks now and then with held-in sighs. Finally he said, "Scott's dropped out of college."

"Already?"

My father nodded slowly. He went on talking amid many pauses, as if he were trying to put the matter as precisely as possible. "He called me at the office today . . . Said 'Papa, I'm sorry' . . . And I said 'What, son? It can't be all that bad' . . . Said he hadn't been going to classes, and now he didn't really see the point. I asked"—he frowned deeply, pushing his bottom lip out—"I asked him, 'What's wrong, son? What's the matter?' . . . 'I don't know, Papa.' " My father shrugged and repeated, in Scott's woebegone way, " 'I don't know.' "

My father was staring intently at the curdled surface of his cream of mushroom soup. His face was turning red. I couldn't think of anything to say.

"Is the tuition refundable," I asked finally, "or what?"

He covered his eyes and shook his head. He didn't bury his face in his hands—that would have been too embarrassing—but just pressed his fingers hard against his forehead while his face froze into a proud, trembling frown. I'd never seen him cry and knew he didn't want me to sit there and watch. I stood up, kissed the top of his burning forehead, and left the room.

MY BROTHER'S FEES were paid until the end of the semester, so he went on living in the dorm a while. He was something of a legend there, for the usual reasons only more so. The NYU authorities had asked him to leave after various infractions, but Scott wouldn't cooperate. The stalemate persisted a few days, until finally they managed to eject him, bodily ("Get your fucking hands off me, man!"), and wouldn't even let him return to collect his trunk.

So things stood when Marlies flew to New York in an effort to settle her son's affairs. She and Burck had decided to send him to Germany, in hopes that my grandfather, a psychiatrist, could somehow figure him out. Indeed, both my grandparents were nothing but eager to help. They remembered Scott as the solemn, sensitive boy in a blazer and clip-on necktie who'd nursed his sick mother aboard the *Nieuw Amsterdam*, as the moody but still tractable lad they'd seen a few years later, at age thirteen, when he'd gone abroad all by himself and learned to speak German after a fashion. My grandmother, a great-souled woman, had fretted over reports of Scott's problems and was full of advice for her wayward daughter, who was thus inspired to say, in so many words: *He's all yours.*

And so the stage was set for the biggest fiasco yet. When my mother arrived in New York—it was Saturday, the day before Scott's scheduled departure for Germany—he told her with considerable bitterness that they wouldn't let him back in the dorm to collect his fucking stuff, etc. My mother agreed to take care of it, and asked Scott to wait outside. This he refused to do. In the lobby was a security guard who, for all we know, had been specifically retained to bar his entrance. These two began to scuffle, while my mother screamed at Scott to get the hell out of there. Abruptly he seemed to obey, shoving free of the guard and walking, with scornful dignity, out the door, then breaking into a giddy little scamper around the building (my mother in hot pursuit) to a glass door in back. Locked. Without a whit of reflection, Scott stepped back, lowered his shoulder, and crashed through the glass.

William Maxwell once wrote, "New York City is a place where one can weep on the sidewalk in perfect privacy," and that day my mother learned just how right he was. Walking uptown through the Village—past old haunts, the places where she'd been so happy and sad, burning her candle at both ends à la Edna St. Vincent Millay, arguing about Ayn Rand and Camus and the like—she wept and wept. Wailing away, a weaving gait. Weeping, weeping, all the way back to the Hotel Chelsea, all the way up in the elevator, all the way down to the restaurant, where the waiter could scarcely help but notice her distress and kindly plied her with liquor ("not a good idea," she recalled). Later she got a message from the concierge: Call Precinct Eight. Whereupon she was told that her son was uninjured but naturally in jail and would appear before the judge at nine o'clock in the morning. On Sunday? Oh yes, seven days a week. And so the next morning my mother appeared in court and presented the judge with Scott's plane ticket for a two o'clock flight to Germany; the miscreant was lectured and let go with a warning.

By then the pot and drugs and drink had metabolized somewhat, and Scott was contrite. He agreed to go to a barber and get a respectable haircut prior to his departure. The door-smashing episode had caused a further stir in his dorm, and Scott's three suitemates were eager to accompany him and my mother to the airport. She made this gleeful trio wait with her at the gate until her son's plane was unmistakably in the air, then breathed "a humongous sigh of relief" and invited them all to dinner at the Chelsea. Theirs was a merry table—the same table, it so happened, where she'd been so inconsolable the night before, and the same waiter, who was glad to see her feeling better. Later she and the boys sat around on her bed, drinking and laughing about the whole incredibly fucked-up mess. The guys thought it was wild that Scott, that crazy fucker, had such a cool mom.

I HEARD A few things about Scott's time in Germany, but the rest is speculation. The one photograph is telling: he is slouched between my grandparents, laughing, arms flung over their shoulders; my grandfather, propped stiffly against his metal cane, shares nothing of Scott's mirth; my grandmother clutches her purse and deplores Scott with a look of stern, melting love. She adored him and vice versa. Her babbling admonitions to be good and go to church seemed to soothe him. He'd sit passive and smiling while she brought him food and insisted on rubbing his pimply face with some kind of ointment that had worked for her as a girl. Both of them reproached my grandfather, whose exasperation was such that he became the weary embodiment of Wittgenstein's dictum, "Whereof one cannot speak, one must be silent." As the head of an asylum, Opa had been around lunacy all his life and sympathized up to a point: during the war he'd saved a number of patients by alerting their families to come take them home and hide them from the Nazis. His own son, my uncle Richard, had been a little off when young (low grades, a dazed loutish look), and now was a clubby bearded burgher who sold neon signs.

As for Scott, poor Opa could hardly believe what a difference five years had wrought. What had become of his *lieber Sohn*? Who was this sullen *Tage Dieb* ("day thief" or "wastrel")? Asked not to play his music so loud, Scott would lock himself in Opa's study with a cache of liquor and blast the Ramones. This went on for a month, maybe, until Opa called Richard, who yanked my brother to his feet, slapped him around a bit, and told him to get his ass on a plane. Oma saw him off at the gate, weeping.

WHEN SCOTT CAME home for Christmas he looked ghastly. His face was boiling with pimples, pimples on top of pimples, and his hair hung like a pair of dank curtains one wouldn't care to part. He seemed weirdly cheerful withal. Between Germany and Oklahoma he'd stopped in New York for a couple of weeks, basically living on the street and somehow managing to stuff himself with drugs enough to last into the new year. Or so I assumed, since he didn't appear to be getting high in our house. But who knows.

All I knew was that every time he opened his mouth something strange came out, as though he were addressing us from the fog of some alien world.

That first day home he came into my room and sat on the floor. After a few inconclusive exchanges, he fell silent and began surveying every detail of his surroundings, his head rolling around on his shoulders, slowly, like a security camera. Finally his eyes fixed on me.

"Your face . . ." he said, after almost a full minute of scrutiny, during which I'd tried to seem oblivious and then said "*What?*" a number of times. "It's all—kind of fucked up . . ."

Look who's talking, I thought. "How so?"

"Your nose is like"—he stared hard, trying to fathom it—"I don't know, Zwieb, it's like *asymmetrical* and shit . . ."

Actually my nose is fairly straight, or at least it was in those days. "Really?"

"Yeah!" And he went on staring while his hand traced ineffable shapes in the air that were meant to approximate my nose. He wasn't trying to be offensive so much as helping me see what he saw.

Mostly Scott embarrassed me. I was fifteen, puberty had kicked in at last, and I wanted nothing more than to be normal—that is, as unlike my brother as possible. I didn't want anyone to see us together, to guess we were brothers, and I couldn't understand why my father would invite both of us downtown for lunch. But there he was, my father, natty in a tailored gray suit, striding out of his office and hugging my ragamuffin brother for all to see: a modern-dress Prodigal Son. The odd colleague would drift into our ken and pause with a barely perceptible start as he or she recognized Scott and absorbed, smiling, whatever Martian pleasantry he made. "Hey, Terry," Scott said to one of them in an intense half-whisper, as if he were mimicking the sort of self-assured big-shot who could affect such intimacy and get away with it. "How's the wife? You're looking very . . . healthy." Burck's expression at such times was fixed, inscrutable, with perhaps a shimmer of misery underneath.

We spent Christmas Day with Oma from Vinita. She'd broken her hip the month before, and my father had brought her to Oklahoma City to recuperate in one of the nicer rest homes. Her roommate was a crazy old mummy named Tula who delighted in tormenting her: Tula threw food at my grandmother and once, slyly, left a bedpan full of coy turds on their common bedside table. (Marlies—who had a very German fondness for scatological humor and a rather strained relationship with her mother-in-law—adored Tula.) In short, Oma was having a bad time of it, and I wondered if she might be spared the sight of my brother.

But we were a family, after all. So we sat around taking pictures and opening presents in that gloomy, yellow-curtained common room. Scott was creepily solicitous toward Oma, kneeling at the foot of her wheelchair and caressing her shrunken shoulder, while my parents smiled and I looked on with a kind of cringing bemusement. Oma returned Scott's tenderness by touching a trembling hand to his pimply cheek, his arm, as though she were trying to palpate the precious boy within.

I thought of my favorite Christmas, eight years before. Oma was visiting, and Scott decided to put on a show for her and our parents. Before we opened presents on Christmas Eve, my brother and I sang and danced and did a skit in identical blue pajamas. The highlight was my reading of "A Visit from St. Nicholas" accompanied by my Pooh bear, who was dressed in a vest and bow tie and seated beside me on a bar stool. We alternated lines: I read mine with an orotund flourish, while Pooh muttered his in a bear-voice I'd practiced all week. We were a hit. I can still see Oma—who often smiled but rarely laughed (because of her teeth?)—clutching her son's shoulder with gasping hilarity. There's a photo of me taking a deep bow afterward while Scott, beaming, stands behind me. The show had been his idea, and he was proud of me.

AS MUCH AS possible I stayed away while Scott was home. What galled me most was not that Scott himself was oblivious to his condition, but that my parents too seemed bent on pretending that nothing much was amiss, that time would heal. They doted on Scott in my presence, as if to rebuke me for failing, balefully, to do my part. But I couldn't help it. The sight of Scott struck me dumb; I was terrified of turning into him.

One morning he came into the bathroom while I was washing my face—still pretty clear at the time—and said he wanted to watch, that perhaps he was doing something *wrong* to have so many pimples. It occurs to me now that he was just trying to find something for us to talk about.

"Well, there's nothing much *to* it," I said with faint exasperation, with the kind of stoical condescension one shows a pestering six-year-old. If my brother caught on to this, he gave no sign; the year before he would have clouted me upside the head. Now he just stood there, lips parted, while I covered my face with Noxzema and washed it off with a hand towel and hot water.

That was the last I saw of Scott for a long time. For a week or so I contrived to stay away at friends' houses, and one day when I came home to change clothes, Scott was gone. He'd decided to go back to New York for no particular reason.

THAT WAS THE year my parents' marriage, long moribund, came to an end. They still had moments of companionship, but mostly they led separate lives. Even when my mother was home she slept alone in my old bedroom, which she'd converted into a kind of Arabic caravansary—a low brass table with elaborate pewter pitchers, tapestries of desert scenes, and the like. But the whole Arabic thing had palled, and I imagine such decor served only as a bleak reminder of certain failed experiments. Little wonder she preferred life in Norman: most of her stuff was there, and she'd taken up with a tall, baby-faced grad student, Dave, who helped her care for some famous chimps who knew sign language.

On the surface, at least, my father grudged her nothing: for a long time she'd been unhappy—despite the seeming festivity of her life—and now she was somewhat better. Besides, Burck was doing his own thing as well. That summer he went to Colorado for an Outward Bound program. Slender enough to begin with, he returned several pounds lighter and glowed with idealistic notions of a better life: more simplicity, more reflection, fewer "poisons" such as coffee and alcohol (which he'd never consumed to excess anyway). He showed me a photo of his Outward Bound group, all of them happily bedraggled after their long ordeal in the mountains; Burck was the oldest by far (forty-five), but his smudged and grinning face was boyish. That summer, too, he spent a month or so with a family in Sweden. The mother was a big woman in her late thirties named Elsie, who'd met my father while touring the States with an avant-garde acting troupe. She was the type who sensed "connections" with certain people—correctly so in my father's case. A couple of years later, I too visited Elsie's family in Sweden, and they spoke of Burck as an almost holy figure—so kind and curious and fun. They showed me a drawing that the little girl had made of my father in a diving pose at the village lake. By comparison I was a big disappointment: a glum, self-conscious adolescent, I was taken aback by Elsie's persistent wish to discuss things like masturbation; also (to my later shame) I showed little interest in getting to know her daughter, then a shy thirteen-year-old who didn't speak much English and was rather plain. For my father, though, it was a liberation of sorts. Not long ago I found some letters he'd written my mother from Sweden, all about how hopeful he was for a renascent marriage on his return.

AMONG MY FATHER'S resolves that fall was to rescue Scott from New York. My brother's letters and occasional phone calls had become increasingly bizarre, all the more for being fairly articulate. With a lot of elaborate wordplay he described all the "crazy moothray fookrays" that one encounters in the course of a long, idle day in the city. A bum in Tompkins Square had put a knife to Scott's throat and demanded a blow job; certain people, normal-seeming to begin with, had beaten the shit out of him "for no reason." He was persecuted on all sides but, with a kind of wan bravado, insisted he was happy. New York was the only town for him.

Burck went to an address in Hell's Kitchen indicated by Scott's letters. I picture him standing on the sidewalk in his suede blazer and loafers, the rabble reeling around him as he glances from an envelope to a squalid tenement and back to the envelope again. Scott's apartment was several flights up; perhaps there were a few sunburned, shirtless junkies asleep on the stairs. Though my father had alerted Scott to his visit—writing well in advance and specifying date and time—Scott wasn't expecting him. He received my father warmly but had a hard time staying awake. A pair of checked, institutional-looking trousers hung loose and filthy around Scott's bony pelvis; a patchy beard sprouted amid the pimples. At some point he began talking about a Utopian society he wanted to found on the bottom of the sea. My father offered to pay his way home on the condition that he see a psychiatrist, kick the drugs, and go back to school (or get a job), in that order, but Scott wasn't ready yet. He thanked him all the same.

My father told me about this visit only once, some twenty years later, and I may be misremembering certain details. By then we only spoke of Scott once or twice a year, while a kind of gas filled the room until we could barely breathe unless we changed the subject. Before that happened, usually, either he or I would have found some fresh detail or story, a bit of colored glass to add to the mosaic of my brother's life. It was a work in progress on our part.

MY MOTHER'S LIFE in Norman was purposeful and pleasant, a relief from "the fugitive distress of hedonism," as Cyril Connolly would have it. Her visits home, with us, became more and more a matter of duty. For a long time she'd craved escape from the chaos of Scott's presence, but now the house seemed, if anything, rather forlorn and pointless. I myself was rarely around; I resented her desertion and almost made a point of keeping away during her rare visits. Our dogs were dead. As for my parents' marriage: since Sweden they'd adopted a greater openness, a kind of enforced candor that entailed discussing their love lives in elaborately casual detail.

For Marlies, then, coming home meant getting drunk with old friends who'd long ago begun to bore her. One day she and Phyllis ("*Chlo-eeee!*") and Marilyn (an alcoholic doctor) and Marilyn's brother (the proprietor of a scuba shop) were having a long boozy lunch in the basement of the Tiffany House apartments near the intersection of May Avenue and Northwest Expressway. I'm unsure what the Tiffany House looked like in 1979; nowadays it's pretty grim, part of the nondescript suburban badlands—a painting by the misanthropic love-child of Norman Rockwell and de Chirico. After three or four hours in the Tiffany House, the scuba guy said he needed to get back to his shop, and Marlies offered him a lift. It was only a mile or so. They were sailing along in her massive Caddy when the guy said his shop was coming up on the right, so Marlies abruptly turned right and sideswiped a woman trying to pass. My mother drifted back into the left lane, waited for what she would always insist was a seemly interval, then swerved right again—"and lo and behold," she remembers (indignant unto the present day), "that damn broad was there again!" They all pulled into a parking lot, and the scuba guy went into his shop and called the police, whom Marlies berated, gaily, from the backseat of their squad car ("for catching me instead of the stupid broad that insisted on passing me even though she could clearly see that I was trying to make a turn into the right lane . . ."). She also begged for cigarettes, but the stolid cops wouldn't budge, explaining that it would affect her Breathalyzer test. "All the more reason!" she cackled. Later, in jail, she managed to bum a smoke from her cellmate—a weeping woman who'd been caught stealing from the Dollar General—and used the smoldering match to write "Marlies slept here" on the underside of her cellmate's cot.

Four hours later my father arrived. "What kept you so long?" my mother snapped at him, and Burck calmly replied that he'd considered leaving her there overnight in hopes of teaching her a lesson. Otherwise he didn't reproach her. Indeed, he was glad to be of use. He hired an old friend to handle her case, a man whose alcoholism (then in abeyance) had left him somewhat washed up as a lawyer. He was glad for the work but didn't do a very good job, according to Marlies, whose license was revoked for a year; she was also ordered to attend six months of AA meetings and take a course about drinking and driving. The first part of her punishment made her furious.

"Now you *do* something!" she scolded my father. "You get the nastiest crooks off, so you just see to it I don't lose my license!"

And Burck handled that too—gladly, again, but I think in a quiet way he'd decided that enough was enough. He wanted a different kind of life, and so in spades did Marlies, who cheerfully attended her AA meetings (a hilarious chapter of mostly gay men) and found the drinking-and-driving course "very informative." But none of it, really, was necessary by then. Marlies was through with all that, or anyway the worst of it—the daily tippling and dreary repetitive jokes, the Arabic youths, the Free Spirit, the whole scene. She devoted herself all the more to her studies.

One day I came home and found my parents sitting together on the living room couch. Burck was caressing Marlies's hands in his lap, and they looked at each other with an earnestness that somehow excluded me.

"It's good we can talk this way," said my father, letting her hand go with a quick pat (wrapping it up) and greeting me with a smile. It was over.

part II

weeds don't die

got my driver's license around the time of my parents' divorce, and promptly began to follow in Scott and Marlies' wavering tire tracks. It didn't help that I too liked to get drunk, or that my father traveled a fair amount and trusted me too much. Once I took his silver Sedan de Ville for a joyride and dented the rim of the right front wheel by swerving over a curb. I managed to replace it from a salvage yard, rather cheaply and in the nick of time, quite pleased by how I'd handled the matter. The morning after my father's return, however, he called me outside in an ominously even voice. He stood peering into the open trunk. "Has someone been in this trunk?" he asked. "No," I lied; "why?" He invited me to have a look inside, where he'd stowed a number of museum prints prior to framing; the cut-rate grease monkey I'd hired had crumpled these up and thrust them into the tire well. "Has someone been in this trunk?" he repeated. "I guess so," I said, affecting amazement.

Around that time, too, I smashed up my own first car, a 1975 Vega hatchback that I'd had for all of two months ("the snatch hatch" I roguishly named it, with scant reason). Late for school one morning, I'd briskly scraped some ice off the windshield, which refroze within a block of our house; rather than pull over and do a better scraping job, I blindly plowed into a neighbor's parked car. I returned to our house on foot and summoned my father. He stood there in the street, dressed for work in an elegant navy suit and camel's-hair topcoat, surveying the two demolished vehicles with practiced detachment. "The joys of fatherhood," he remarked.

Burck tried to be stoical toward my more serious lapses, but otherwise seemed in a state of constant, seething irritation where I was concerned. Not without cause. My everyday attitude was a bit on the blasé side. Toward money, for instance. In the middle drawer of his desk he kept a checkbook, of which I availed myself when I needed small amounts of cash. I kept forgetting (often on purpose) to record my withdrawals and was called on the carpet once a month to explain the discrepant balance. Also, we bought our groceries from an upscale neighborhood market where my father had a charge account; I ignored the fruits and vegetables, deli meats, and good bread he bought, in favor of gourmet frozen meals that I charged by the cartful and ate for breakfast, lunch, and dinner. "Why don't you eat this stuff?" Burck demanded, standing beside the fridge and waving a baguette in my face while I somberly ate a fat lasagna for my afternoon snack. "Is it because you're too goddamn *lazy* to fix a sandwich? Because the best you can do is press a button on the microwave?" That was it in a nut-shell, though I sat there in wounded silence, heartily sick of being persecuted over trifles.

At the time I felt more sinned against than sinning. I didn't have a single close friend whose parents were divorced, and to some extent I blamed my father for our sad, anomalous bachelor arrangement: he shouldn't have let his wife run wild like that, and God knows what-all he should have done about Scott. Since it was out of the question to say so (and since on some level I knew better), I avoided my father as much as possible. If he joined me in front of the TV of an evening, I'd let a decorous five minutes pass before mutely leaving the room. If he nagged me about my dirty dishes in the sink—or any number of cumulative misdemeanors—I'd slowly get up and take care of it with a look of haggard martyr-dom. At least once I gave vent to my bitterness.

"I can't do anything right! It's gotten to where I hate being here!"

I meant this to sting. I wanted my father to feel contrite.

"Then *leave*," he said. "Pack your shit and get out. Go find an apartment and live there. I'll be happy to pay your rent." And he went on to enumerate the many ways I'd made him feel unloved and alone these past few months, though of course he didn't put it in those words. And while it hurts me to remember this, I was relatively unmoved at the time. Perhaps in the abstract it struck me as a shame that we, who'd been so close, didn't get along any-more, but I thought he'd made a botch of our lives and deserved to suffer for it.

Still, I had to go on living there—taking my own apartment would have been even more stigmatizing than the present arrangement —so later that evening I conceded I'd been less than an ideal housemate. "I'm sorry," I said. "I love and respect you more than any person on earth."

Burck accepted this lame, mawkish apology with a nod and went back to his reading.

ONE EVENING HE told me, rather irritably in passing, that my brother's bus would arrive that night from New York; he wanted me to give Scott a ride to a friend's apartment (Todd the Tortoise's apartment, it turned out). I hadn't seen Scott in sixteen months and felt no eagerness to see him now. I don't think I registered any emotion one way or the other on learning that he was, for whatever reason, returning from New York; it's possible I was a little annoyed at having it sprung on me like that. Anyway, I told my father I was meeting a friend that night.

My father lowered his newspaper and looked at me bleakly. "Then you and your friend drive to the bus station at ten thirty-five and pick up your brother." He gave the newspaper a sharp flick and resumed reading.

Though my brother looked different, I was able to spot him from a fair distance among the shabby stragglers standing outside the station. He'd cropped his hair short for his homecoming, and his face looked older, peevish—I was fifteen minutes late—but his manner of bouncing on his toes and staring around with an arrogant upturned chin was unmistakable. He was wearing his checked trousers and a yellowing white T-shirt. I didn't get out of the car, so there was no question of our hugging each other. The disinclination was mutual, I think, as I hadn't answered more than two or three of his letters, long ago, and then in a perfunctory, pompous way. I was never home when he called.

He nodded at my friend—they knew each other slightly—and tossed his duffel bag in the backseat. No more steamer trunk. He

glared out the window while I tried catching his eye in the rearview mirror. I asked for an address.

He ignored this. He wanted to know what I thought of our
parents. He meant the divorce.

"What do you mean?" I said, with pointed annoyance. I didn't
want to discuss the divorce around my friend. I hadn't told him or
anybody else about it.

My brother, just as pointedly, spelled it out—that is, he picked
up on the fact that I didn't want to discuss it, and why, and was
therefore all the more determined to do so. "The *divorce*," he said.

"What about it?"

He shook his head. I asked him again for some kind of address;
I was driving aimlessly around the block in one of the worst parts
of the city. My friend—a tense young man who ironed his own
shirts—kept his eyes averted and pursed his lips.

"You don't care at all, do you?" said Scott.

"As a matter of fact, I don't. As a matter of fact, Scott, I thought
the marriage was a joke and I'm *glad* it's over."

This wasn't true, though at the time I thought it should have
been. In fact, when my father finally got around to telling me
about it, I professed in somewhat milder terms to think it best for
all concerned. If I showed any bitterness at all, it was against my
absentee mother: "I assume there won't be any turbulent custody
battle," I said. My father relayed this remark to her on the phone
and they both laughed, relieved I was taking it so well. I'd wanted
them to be hurt by my seeming indifference.

"Okay?" I said to Scott in the rearview mirror.

He wouldn't look at me. He was staring out the window.

"*Address?*"

He let a few beats pass, then gave me his destination with a
sort of desolate petulance. It wasn't far.

"Thanks for the ride," he said, getting out.

I watched him go. Beyond my friend's blurred profile—staring straight ahead—I saw Scott mount the stairs of a mud-colored stucco building that looked vacant, condemned, except for a weak yellow lightbulb over the front door. My brother stood waiting in that light, hugging his duffel bag, until finally his friend stuck a wary, disheveled head out. The head withdrew, the door stayed open, and my brother held up one stiff hand and waved it, for me, before walking inside.

My friend and I went our way without a word on the subject of Scott or my parents' divorce, as if the whole ten-minute episode had been a dream.

I WAS ALMOST expelled from school that year. I didn't even know I was in trouble. Though I'd always been a bit of a behavior problem—the *benign* kind, I liked to think: a loudmouth, a clown, a showoff, but sort of endearing too—I was honestly at a loss when my father called me that afternoon from his office. He sounded very angry. He kept his voice down almost to a whisper, which was all the more menacing in its modulated intensity.

"Your vice principal just called. Said they're about *this* close to throwing your ass out of there for good. We have to go to a disciplinary conference tomorrow. Meanwhile you're suspended for three days."

"But why?"

"Now you listen to me—" His voice dropped a notch further. "You listen *real* good, son. I been through this shit once. Not gonna do it again. I'll send your sorry ass to military school. You write that down. You put that on a piece of paper."

"I don't—"

But he'd already hung up.

This, then, was the otherwise unspoken theme of my father's peevishness toward me: he wouldn't tolerate another Scott. It was so unfair. I'd had *one* major car wreck, in a crappy five-year-old Vega; Scott had blithely battered his Porsche—his Porsche!— four or five times, and my father had paid for its repair all but once. And yes, I drank a lot of beer, but I wasn't on drugs. I was a mediocre student, but I did maintain a decent B average. I was moody and self-absorbed, but I was basically sane. My friends were the most mainstream, regular bunch in school. In short I was doing *great*, just great, at least when you considered that my brother was nuts, my mother had abandoned us, and my father picked at my every picayune flaw.

That night we avoided each other. I sat in my room and rehearsed, with scalding eyes, all the scathing things I'd say to my persecutors; my father was too tired and disgusted to talk to me. The next morning, when he drove us to school, his manner was subdued. He asked me what it was all about, and I told him I had no idea. He seemed to accept this, nodding, and we didn't speak again.

Brother Howie, the vice principal, was a pale, squat, square-shaped man in a black polyester suit. He blinked behind wire-rim glasses in a flustered, tic-ish way as he shook hands with my father. By contrast my father seemed princely—gracious, receptive, vividly prosperous, and subtly annoyed that his time had been given up to such proceedings. He kept his head cocked gravely and waited for Brother Howie to explain.

The deal, said Howie, was this: I hadn't done anything *major*, but a number of teachers had come to him with "concerns"— three on the same day, in fact, which had "raised a red flag." He thought it best, then, that they "nip this thing in the bud," if possible. My father nodded.

A couple of teachers took the time to come in and discuss their concerns, and I was dejected but unsurprised to find that these were my favorite teachers. There was Mr. Bernard, the music teacher who'd ordered porn and Jack Daniel's up to his room at the Hyatt during our band trip to New Orleans. His everyday manner was ironical and tolerant. While helping to paint sets for the play, he told my father, I'd carelessly spattered paint all over the floor of the band room and made no effort to clean it up. My face burned with anger and shame: anger because I'd been kicked out of the cast of that play, in light of which I thought it magnanimous of me to work on those sets at all, and shame because the nature of my offense was all too similar to what my father dealt with on a daily basis. But he said nothing and neither did I. Next was my drama teacher, Ms. Archer, the woman who'd kicked me out of the play. The previous summer, with two of my friends, Ms. Archer had traveled a hundred miles to watch me perform at a prestigious arts camp. On the way she'd gotten drunk and given one of my friends a hand job in the back of a van. Since then she'd been subject to weird mood swings and paranoia (when touched from behind she'd jump as if Tasered), in the midst of which she'd kicked me out of that play, because I'd asked—snidely, she thought, and once too often—for a little feedback on my performance. To my father she gave a slightly exaggerated account of this episode and related it to the set-painting by way of suggesting a trend; that said, she was moved to add, "Your son knows I love him. He's talented and capable of real brilliance. You know, one moment he's talking about Schopenhauer and the next he's . . ." She bugged her eyes to indicate some typical bit of foolery. I was embarrassed by the reference to Schopenhauer—my father deplored my pseudo-intellectualism, knowing the ignorance at the bottom of it—but mostly I felt betrayed by Ms. Archer, who did love me in a way and was punishing me, I thought, for not loving her enough in return.

Finally Howie added his two cents with a chuckle. I knew what was coming. A couple of weeks before, during lunch, someone had thrown a greasy piece of baked chicken at a sad, shy little girl who always sat alone. For a moment the girl had looked dazed, bereft, then began wiping the grease off her cheek in a slow, tentative way, discreetly dealing with her tears as she did so. Perhaps because I was observing her so intently, and because of my reputation for mischief, the cafeteria monitor had assumed I was the culprit and sent me to Brother Howie's office. I was outraged. I'd been in trouble enough lately without having to answer for something I hadn't done—would *never* have done—so I left a note to that effect on Howie's desk; I wrote that if he "wished to confer" about the matter later, I was happy to oblige, but for now I had to get on to my next class. No sooner had I set foot in this class than Howie's voice, usually so modest and monotone, squawked over the room's intercom speaker demanding my return to the office *now*. He ambushed me in front of the receptionist and three or four students who were getting tardy slips; he seized me by the front of my collarless dress shirt (briefly fashionable then) and shoved me stumbling against the wall. He tore my shirt as he stood there shaking me and telling me what he'd do to me if I ever pulled a stunt like that again.

"*That* got his attention," he told my father, still chuckling in a between-us-men sort of way.

I'd wanted to kill Howie the day he ripped my shirt, or at least do something to defend myself in front of pretty Ms. White, the receptionist. I'd played the scene over and over in my mind: Howie balling up on the floor as I kicked him, or flipping end over end as I pummeled him down the stairs. And here he was bragging to my father.

"I didn't do it," I said. "I didn't throw that"—I paused to swallow the word "fucking"—"chicken."

My voice trembled on the edge of tears, and I fell silent. Everybody but my father was looking at me now with mild reproach, as if to suggest that it wasn't *about* the chicken. My father cleared his throat.

"My son can be difficult," he said, picking his words with care, "but he is, as far as I can tell, without malice. And for reasons I'd rather not go into, both he and I have been through a pretty bad time lately. That's not to excuse his behavior, just to put it in context. I agree with you"—he smiled at Ms. Archer, who nodded with moist eyes—"that he's an exceptional young man. And I can assure you we're going to work on these problems he's having."

The next thing I knew we were on our feet shaking hands. My father's eyes narrowed a bit vis-à-vis Howie, a nuance of contempt I knew well, and then I was free to return to class on a probational basis. I determined to be not only a model student but a model human being, such was my relief on learning that my father hadn't altogether lost his love and respect for me. More than anything related to Scott or my mother, I'd resented him for that.

THIS WAS THE fall of 1980, and my brother was now a twenty-year-old freshman at the University of Oklahoma. After he'd gotten tired of the vagrant life in Manhattan, he assured my father that he was ready to come home and turn over a new leaf, agreeing to all conditions except psychiatric help. "There's nothing wrong with *me*," he said. In return my father bought him a bus ticket and paid his tuition and expenses at OU; he insisted, however, that Scott live in the freshman dormitory, not in the off-campus apartment Scott had wanted because of his relative seniority.

During one of my rare visits chez Marlies, I accepted Scott's invitation to stop by his dorm and say hello. He was delighted to see me. That was the first time it occurred to me that I'd become, effectively, the big brother. Scott *deferred* to me now; what with my careful hair and preppy clothes and circumspect manner (around him), he seemed to accept that I was going places he wasn't likely to go. He'd lost some of his old arrogance, and now he was simply goofy: he bobbed on his toes like a jaybird with a tune stuck in its head. If I said anything remotely odd or droll, he'd screw up his face and let go a burst of elaborate wheezy laughter, slugging me about the chest and shoulders.

That evening he had a date with a girl in his dorm, which was why he particularly wanted me to visit—to show me off to this girl. To show her what a normal, presentable brother he had. What he hadn't counted on was my pimply face, the one sure way of knowing we were brothers. Unaware of the role he wanted me to play, I'd applied a harsh acne cream that dried up the pores and left a flaky white residue that one wasn't supposed to wash off entirely. My brother's eyes kept drifting to the blanched area around my mouth, a bit of localized film, a sight that made his goofy grin flicker slightly. Finally it was time to meet his date, and he came out with it:

"What's that shit on your face, Zwieb?"

I told him. He asked if I minded washing it off, and I said it didn't work if you washed it off, and besides the skin remained white and flaky whether you washed it off or not. My brother was pensive as we started toward the elevators; then he ducked into a bathroom and asked me to keep him company. While I stood at the mirror surveying the effects of this wonder drug, Scott came up behind me and rubbed a soapy hand around my mouth.

"Fuck!" I said. "Stop!"

He stopped. "Just *wash* it a little," he pleaded. I splashed a bit of water on my face, raw where he'd rubbed it, and patted it dry with a paper towel. The whiteness returned with a faint, phosphorescent glow.

"See?" I said. "Look: would you rather I meet this girl some other time?"

Scott shook his head with a kind of anxious, haunted look. The rest of me was *fine*, he said, and indicated as much by plucking the shoulders of my button-down shirt and skimming a hand over the gloss of my careful hair. The fullness of pride leaked from his eyes.

The girl was a decided anticlimax. She'd set up an ironing board in the hall outside her room and was dank with toil. Blowzy and moonfaced, she put me in mind of a good-natured housemaid who tells your kids about Jesus while scrubbing the toilets. Nor would she have been out of place in a Vermeer, hefting a milk jug.

"Scott, this your bruth-uh?" she said with an Okie drawl. She shook my hand over the ironing board, glancing at the film around my mouth and smiling a little too brightly. "He just talks and talks about *yew!*"

"Well," I said, "and vice versa."

"I look awful! *Scawwt!*"

Scott mumbled something about her looking fine, *beautiful* in fact, this in a husky reverential way that made her (and me) blush. Then the girl shot me a look to let me know she wasn't really *serious* about Scott, that she was just being—*you* know—nice, but it was good to meet me anyway. All that with a quick little smirk.

"What'd you think, Zwieb?" my brother asked as we parted in the lobby.

"She's nice," I said, and gave him a hug. "But maybe not your type?"

He began to say something, but thought better of it. He gave me an unhappy smile and went back to the elevator.

"How was Scott?" my father asked that night.

I said he seemed all right. And it may have been that same weekend that I had an interesting exchange with some incidental numbskull at a keg party. He was a college student, and I was about to be a college student.

"What'd you say your name was?" he asked.

I told him, and with a drunken hoot the guy said he *thought* so, that the craziest motherfucker he'd ever met in his whole mother-fucking life went by that name and kind of looked like me too; people on his floor called him "the punk rocker" 'cause all he ever did was get wasted and listen to the Ramones and shit. My interlocutor bugged his eyes and mimed sucking a joint, bouncing in place like a jaybird with a tune stuck in its head. Did I have a brother like that?

I did not.

"Shit, I bet you do!" he said, backing away, spritzing a jet of beer between his grinning front teeth.

AND SO, MY father beside me, I sat on a sagging couch a month or two later and watched my brother bounce around to a B-52s record in the grim apartment he took when he dropped out of college again and moved back to Todd the Tortoise's neighbor-hood in the bleakest section of downtown Oklahoma City—a slum of crumbling bungalows, apartment houses that looked like Aztec ruins, and the odd vacant lot of overgrown grass and trash

and dog shit. On the whole he seemed happier: through old connections he'd gotten a job in a good restaurant—busing tables
for now, with the possibility of becoming a waiter if he "worked
out"—and here, amid these stained and fissured walls, he could
bounce around to his heart's content. Apparently he'd spent a lot
of time at CBGB's and the like in New York, where such behavior was hardly out of the ordinary. My father kept him company
with a jiggling foot, an indulgent smile. Scott was on his own
again, this was his apartment, and he could carry on howsoever
he liked. He was free, white, and almost twenty-one.

Back in the car, Burck sat a moment before starting the
engine. A smile lingered on his face like a door he'd forgotten
to shut. "Scott is strange," he said, "but in many ways . . ." He
peered up at Scott's window and frowned. "In many ways he's a
very lovable young man."

The worst part was watching my father parry the questions of
a curious public. He was a well-known man. On the street, in
crowded restaurants, striding through the carpeted underground
tunnels downtown, he was accosted: "And how's that *older* boy
of yours? What's *he* up to these days?" Around me, at least, he
couldn't equivocate, and I doubt he could anyway; for all his
surface polish, he never became adept at handling that particular question. Perhaps he never meant to. Rather he *taught* these
acquaintances, one by one, never to repeat their error. Wincing
as if lashed, he'd muster a faint smile—puzzled at the world's
obtuseness—and say in a soft voice, "Well . . . I don't really know,
Ted. Have to get back to you on that."

THE MAIN REASON my parents had gone to the trouble of
formalizing a divorce was because my father had fallen in love.

Her name was Mandy, and she was exactly half his age, a law student at OU who'd clerked in his firm the summer before my senior year in high school—for me a summer of long enforced walks around the neighborhood, of loitering with friends, because Mandy was visiting and I'd been tacitly banished, another source of friction between Burck and me.

But I liked Mandy. There was nothing not to like: she was sweet, she was smart, and while perhaps not a beauty, she had a cute little body and a big toothy grin; her whole face and neck would flush when she looked at my father, whom she wanted to screw almost every waking minute of the day and night. For him this wasn't a problem. Sometimes, though, he had to work or whatever, and after her clerkship was over Mandy and I played a lot of afternoon racquetball. We were pals. I found myself missing her when she left for Scotland that fall on a Rotary law scholarship; except for the constant walking on my part, she'd made our home a happier place.

As for those walks . . . they served a purpose, perhaps. I took them sometimes very early in the morning, in the powdery twilight, and sometimes at night when our neighbors' interior lights were on and I got little glimpses of how other lives were led. And how did I aspire to live myself? That question would hang in the air for many years.

As one walked east from our house on the corner of Wilshire and Dorset—again with the English street names, far more suitable in Nichols Hills than in our shabby old tract-house neighborhood, the Village—the houses gradually and almost aggressively became grander. Gatsby's mansion in West Egg is described as "a factual imitation of some Hôtel de Ville in Normandy," and this would not have been out of place (indeed, when Nichols Hills was founded in 1929—so I just now read on the town's website—the entrance at the corner of 63rd and Western was marked by "two stately towers of true Normandy architecture"); because the curving, park-dotted streets had been laid along sumptuous prairie north of the city, there was much in the way of vast, Gatsby-esque "blue lawns" as well. The Oklahoma City Golf & Country Club was only a few blocks away from our house: it was pleasant to walk along the golf-cart paths at dawn, cheered by birdsong and the warble of little speakers concealed in the trees that played Muzak around the clock. The clubhouse itself was a sprawling Tudor, further east of which, the sky brightening, was an almost bumptious parade of prosperity—not just Normandy mansions such as Gatsby and Dr. Nichols had inhabited, but Greek Revivals, Georgians, Spanish Colonials, glassy Modernist castles, or composites of all these styles and more, a gallimaufry reminiscent of Nathanael West's Hollywood. At Christmas the light displays were competitively dazzling.

So I walked those many mornings and nights. And yes, part of me coveted the big houses, the verdant neighborhood, the never having to protest too much about one's little importance in the world. But part of me could also see—could see very easily—a different kind of life: a little garret apartment, say, in some other part of the world, with nothing but books and a few souvenirs of the oddball life I'd led, and perhaps an occasional lapse into real squalor from time to time. Given my vagaries, it was all possible—the high and low and in-between.

WHEN MANDY RETURNED from Edinburgh for a month over the holidays, I was amiably tolerated but encouraged, as ever, to make myself scarce. There was no question of my celebrating Christmas with them. My mother, whom I'd seen maybe five times in the past year, stepped obligingly to the fore. She too liked Mandy (or the idea of her), and in the interest of giving the happy couple their privacy, she gladly invited me and my brother to spend Christmas at her little condo in Norman. I viewed the prospect as one might view a bit of court-imposed community service, to be performed in a rest home or hospital. Christmas was the one time I couldn't depend on friends; Christmas was family, of whatever sort.

For some reason my brother drove. He'd recently bought (with my father's help) a big tan Oldsmobile that rumbled with a kind of elderly resolve when Scott stepped on the gas. His old twill cap, I noticed, had somehow survived New York, and he'd adjust the bill with a little flourish each time we slowly gathered speed after a stoplight. An aspect of my brother's evolving, quasi-adult persona was a heavy pair of horn-rim glasses that lent him a kind of comic dignity; he'd been a little nearsighted since his early teens, though he'd usually worn contacts to spare his then-handsome face. Now, with his cap and glasses and trench coat, his smile of vague importance as he chauffeured us to Norman, he gave me the sense of playing a minor role in a costume farce.

My mother and Scott brought out, if not exactly the worst, the weirdest in each other. Starved for love, Scott would follow her around her tiny condo, her little garden, finding excuses to hug and kiss and caress her. I suppose my mother did her best to reciprocate, but she wasn't a patient woman, and Scott was pathetic in a thousand ways. Besides, she was trying to *cook*, and Scott would hover and hover around her tiny kitchen until she groaned with exasperation. "Scott, will you get *outta* here?" she'd finally explode, waving her wooden spoon and bugging her eyes. And Scott would join me on the couch and sullenly sip his beer, his umpteenth strong German beer, which seeped from his eyes and pores while he nursed this latest hurt. Perhaps he'd comfort himself with one of my mother's cats, and here again Scott demanded more from the world than it was ever prepared to give him. Because I ignored the cats they vastly preferred me to Scott, and would writhe free of his clutches and seek refuge in my indifferent lap. Whereupon Scott would sigh and waver to his feet for still another beer. "*Another?*" roared my mother, snapping it out of his hand and returning it to the fridge. "Not until you've eaten something!" On and on they'd argue over a beer and its many implications. Since the result was always the same—Scott would not stop until he got his beer (though maybe he'd consent to "eat something")—I found Marlies's tenacity at least as loony as his.

At this point I'd retreat to my mother's bedroom, where she kept a piano she'd acquired to make me feel more at home during my rare visits (with the result that I played piano rather than talk to her). I relished my solitude while it lasted. Once the argument had petered out in the other room, my brother would join me there at the piano, or rather stand behind me and knead my shoulder with one hand while he held his hard-won beer with the other. He cherished dreams of becoming a rock star—all that bouncing around on his toes was, I believe, by way of regaling a phantom audience. The vocal style he most emulated was that of Led Zeppelin's Robert Plant. I could almost stand hearing "*Stille Nacht*" sung in a nasal falsetto, ditto having my shoulder patted and prodded and probed, but the combination was unsettling, and soon I'd have to end our recital. I would either go for a walk before dinner (the environs included a parking lot and university golf course), watch a bit more TV, or pretend to take a long shit. The last was the only definitely private activity, so there I'd sit while a cat pawed under the door as if begging me to rescue her from Scott.

Dinner was served late in the afternoon. Scott would take his place at the table and survey the victuals with a look of tipsy discernment, then raise a glass to the chef. Their latest brawl momentarily forgotten, Marlies would return the tribute with a kind of sad, proprietary smile, suggesting that Scott was a pain in the ass, all right, but a gracious young man and her own son for better or worse. We'd eat. There was a pork roast, say, with crispy skin and scarlet flesh just so; lovely sweetbreads of an ideal chewiness, never mushy, cooked with mushrooms in a wine sauce; new potatoes and red cabbage and brussels sprouts and a cauliflower steeped in mock hollandaise. My brother would chew each morsel of meat with endless care (eyes fixed on the middle distance), then fastidiously remove the residual fat from his mouth and place it aside, for all to see, on a little plate he'd fetched for that purpose. When I asked him about it—this novel quirk—he explained with old arrogance that he'd rather *not* die of congestive heart failure, thanks. I was about to ask whether he followed the same procedure when eating in public, and (if so) whether he'd ever been denounced as a repulsive idiot, but my mother derailed me by leaning forward on her fists and hissing "Oh Scott, you're so full of *shit*."

After the plates were cleared and the snarling subsided, we decided to go see a movie, a comedy. We had a long night ahead of us, and the thought of spending it, just we three, in that little condo was out of the question. Also it would force my brother to sober up a bit. We wanted to laugh and forget ourselves, however briefly, and few things are more depressing than being thwarted in this simple wish. My brother sprawled between us stinking of beer, not just refusing to laugh but sighing and smacking his lips and scratching his balls (inside the pants), so that a number of people got up and moved. When we got home again and Scott discovered we were out of beer, he started on the Scotch.

At some point he lurched into the bathroom, leaving the door open, and began picking his face. He still had a lot of pimples, the kind that swell beneath the skin and really explode when given a good hard squeeze. Scott kept the door open so he could talk to us the whole time: "You'd think by now this shit would go away . . . How'm I ever gonna get *laid*? . . ."

This went on for almost an hour. At some point my mother asked me, in an urgent whisper, if I wanted to go to midnight mass. I did. Scott heard the sounds of our departure, the zippered coats and jingling keys, and stuck his puckered bleeding face out the door. "Oh," he said, when Marlies explained where we were going. "Save me a wafer."

We hadn't been to church together, my mother and I, since eight years before, when we'd attended midnight mass in Germany with my devout grandparents. Now the place felt like true sanctuary. We arrived early and sang carols with the rest of that wonderfully normal congregation. Marlies embarrassed me by singing in German, or, in the case of "Adeste Fidelis," the original Latin (she deplored the decadent reforms of Vatican Council II). Later, when the priest read the Christmas story, I heard a wet sniffle and knew my mother was letting out the tears she'd held back all day. Finally we went home and found Scott passed out on his stomach by the fireplace, hands tucked under his crotch for warmth like a little boy.

THE NEXT DAY he was churlish with hangover, humiliated after waking up in a dark room with his pimply cheek pressed against the bricks. It didn't help that my mother nagged him ceaselessly, threatening to banish him from the condo until he'd cleaned up his act. Then Scott lost his temper and told her that *she* of all people should talk! I think he called her a cunt at some point (the word was such a normal part of Scott's vocabulary that it didn't really convey the usual nastiness). As ever, of course, Marlies went on giving as good as she got, all to no purpose. I might have tried walking back to my father's house in Oklahoma City had it not been for my mother's boyfriend, Dave—the baby-faced grad student—who joined us for brunch that day. Because his own youth had been somewhat troubled, and because he adored my mother, Dave took special pains to be nice to Scott, and that alone made the rest of the afternoon bearable.

There was one last argument in the parking lot as we were leaving. A few minutes before, my mother had caught Scott sneaking a slug of Scotch on the back porch; he said it was hair of the dog and he'd only had the one, but my mother said it didn't matter— one was all it took!—and demanded he hand over his car keys so I could drive us home. Naturally my brother refused and would go on refusing until the Last Trump, but Marlies stood there berating him all the same and poking her hand out ("Scott: Give . . . me . . . the *keys!*") for a long, long time. Dave stood there holding a camera my mother had asked him to fetch, and finally ended the dispute by snapping a close-up of mother and son in midwrangle. A moment later he took the posed version: my mother standing between us, wan but smiling, vaguely exultant at the prospect of our departure. "Christmas 1980" was her simple but pregnant gloss in the photo album.

From my mother's condo to my father's doorstep took about forty-five minutes in normal traffic, but Scott made it in less than half an hour amid holiday congestion on the interstate. He roared out of my mother's presence and bore down on any motorist who hindered his speed, however innocently; their eyes bugged in their mirrors as they caught sight of the behatted madman in their wake. Scott's only reply to my occasional protests ("*Fuck! . . . Fuck! . . . Slow down, you crazy fucking asshole!*") was to go faster, or rather flex his foot against the already floored gas pedal. Finally we parted without a word in my father's driveway, Scott pausing just long enough for me to step clear.

Burck answered the chain-locked front door in his bathrobe. Flushed and apologetic, he asked me to take a walk, please, and come back in an hour or so.

SHORTLY AFTER MANDY'S return to Scotland, my father began (actually resumed) seeing a woman more or less his own age, Sandra, and soon they decided to marry. Mandy dwindled away amid a welter of tearful transatlantic phone calls, and within a couple of months our lives were entirely different.

Sandra was the antithesis of my mother—they despised each other—and for my father that, I dare say, was the point. Twenty years before, my grandmother and Aunt Kay had thrown a welcoming soirée in Vinita for Burcky's pigtailed, inexplicably German, and quite pregnant bride, who endured perhaps five minutes of polite chitchat with the local hausfrauen before planting herself in front of the TV and watching *Bonanza*. Sandra wouldn't have done that. Indeed, Sandra would have shared the other ladies' consternation in spades, given that she herself was the favorite daughter of Garden City, Kansas, which is perhaps best known for (a) being near Holcomb of *In Cold Blood* fame (Sandra had known the Clutters well) and (b) having the World's Largest Outdoor Municipal Concrete Swimming Pool, which we duly visited, en famille, during our one and only trip to Sandra's hometown. Like my father, Sandra had somewhat transcended her origins: the prettiest girl in her class at Garden City High, and one of the smartest, she'd been Miss Fort Hays State in college and then survived a ghastly first marriage to the local It Boy, a charming narcissist who gave her two gorgeous children: a girl, Kelli, and a son, Aaron, two and eight years younger than I.

Sandra's ménage moved into our house well before the wedding, and forced me to alter those habits that had evolved as a matter of having the place to myself so much. No more lingering bowel movements; now that I shared a bathroom with Kelli, who looked as though she excreted marshmallows, I set my alarm early so I could finish my business in good time and leave the place ventilated once my future stepsister awoke to the song "Celebration," by Kool and the Gang, as she did every wholesome morning for the six months or so before I left for college. In general I had to be less selfish. The little boy, Aaron, was not taking the change well and was often found weeping under somebody's bed; what with his mother at work (public relations) and sister off cheerleading or whatever, it was up to me to coax him out and put him on my knee until he dried up.

Sandra and her children made me feel a bit Caliban-like. Sandra was lovely in a brittle, porcelain sort of way, her strawberry blond hair stylishly coiffed, her frantic smile dissembling some pretty complicated emotional weather. Aaron resembled his mother to an almost unsettling degree, what with his big lashy eyes and rosy cheeks and snub nose (when he went bald at an early age, the effect was that of a depilated Kewpie doll), whereas Kelli was a bosomy, nonbrittle confection of both parents. Back then my stepsiblings seemed not only comelier than I but somewhat sweeter and saner too. A decided liability was my drinking. One memorable evening I was the big loser of a chugging contest, after which I perversely insisted that my friends take me home. This they did, dragging me past the startled eyes of Sandra and her children—Burck too— like a baggy old cadaver crossing the set of *Ozzie and Harriet*.

But if I was Caliban, what did that make my brother? And what would these überkinder make of him? My own feeling was that we should put off that *final* merging of our families as long as possible—at least until Scott's face cleared up and he made the leap to solid citizenhood that one waited for like the spark from heaven. But no. Shortly before the wedding, Scott came to dinner so he could meet his future stepfamily. It could have gone worse. I'm sure that Sandra, determined to help my father by helping his older son, had said something to her kids beforehand, since they twinkled around Scott like social workers in the presence of a promising welfare mother.

"I've eaten there," Kelli gushed, when Scott mentioned his present place of employment. "Oh my God, it's so *good*. It's like the best restaurant in town!"

"Was it fun living in New York?" asked eager Aaron at some point, whereupon his mother broke into a bright smile and said (not for the first time) how *wonderful* it was to be together like this, together at last.

Scott was on his best behavior—that is, a tad creepy but in control, a stylized version of a Nice Young Man. He was careful to enunciate in a way that erased most traces of the slight nasal slur, or blur, the slight drunken quality that had crept into his speech even when sober. When spoken to, he focused on the speaker with walleyed intensity, and toward Kelli, of course, he was courtly to a fault. At such times Scott seemed to sense his old handsomeness like a phantom limb.

After dinner he drew me aside for a private conference. I knew exactly what was coming.

"Have you seen her naked, Zwieb?"

I replied primly—as if the thought had never so much as cast a fluttering shadow across my sun-brightened mind—that she was our *sister* for Christ's sake.

"Stepsister," my brother corrected me. "And they're not married yet." This established, he asked me again if I'd seen her naked, and I said that I hadn't.

SANDRA AND BURCK were married on Good Friday in our living room. A friend of my father presided, a short Polish man who was the most liberal justice on the state supreme court; he seemed very fond of my father, touched to see him so happy, and his voice trembled with old-world sentiment as he performed the ceremony. We children and Oma from Vinita were the only witnesses, and I was the only one who didn't cry a little. I'd volunteered to play Mendelssohn's "Wedding March" at the end, and I stood there worrying about that. My brother's face shined with tears and sebaceous oil. He was wearing a short-sleeved dress shirt and a tie he'd borrowed from our father—come to think of it, that was another reason I was preoccupied: I couldn't help wishing Scott had borrowed a *jacket* too. Sandra and her children had such impeccable fashion sense, and here was my brother looking like an assistant manager at Walmart.

My father was too distracted with happiness to take much notice of my conduct at the crowded reception afterward. While a jazz band played and our guests danced or milled around the caterer's banquet and bar stations, I sat with friends at a table in the farthest corner of our backyard and got plastered. I'd just bounced a quarter into a plastic cup of champagne when Scott summoned me to the opposite side of the yard, where our family was gathering for a photo. He lingered a moment to chat with my friends, most of whom hadn't seen him since high school, and I remember my peevish embarrassment over his bad haircut, complexion, short-sleeved shirt, and slightly off-kilter manner. I was not having fun. I felt like the family pariah. After the ceremony everyone had marched out of the house and left me there, smugly playing Mendelssohn, a random showoff who wasn't trying hard enough to be a good son and brother. Scott, on the other hand, was embraced by all as a kind of philanthropic project, a lovable freak who would prosper in the bosom of a proper family. In that photo we took on the lawn, he occupies the filial place of honor between my father and Oma, while I stand apart with my hands plunged in the pockets of a khaki suit: a tipsy fop at a bus stop. A few minutes later I slipped away with friends to attend Good Friday mass, where I threw up in the vestry. I'd consoled myself that year by becoming a Catholic—more a matter of fitting in with friends, and distancing myself from family, than of spiritual comfort or moral aspiration. In any case it didn't last.

THAT FALL I left for Tulane—a random, even feckless, choice on my part. I knew nobody in New Orleans. I'd submitted one of those "common" applications, and rather than bother with the multiple essays required by better schools (Northwestern, Reed), I figured *What the hell* when Tulane accepted me early. My roommate was a Dutch exchange student named Koenraad van Ginkel, who rarely left our room at Phelps House except to attend meetings of the Karate Club, and who was so broke he ate Cocoa Puffs for breakfast, lunch, and dinner, and would often use my architect's desk lamp by twisting it around on its bolted mount and training it on his side of the room. My other suite-mates were almost as hopeless: a furry little *dese*-and-*dose* guy from Long Island who strutted around in his underwear; two pals from Hollywood, Florida, who wore matching shark-tooth jew-elry; a depressive stoner whose dark room leaked a steady stream

of dope smoke into our common bathroom. With the exception
of Koenraad and me, just about everyone in Phelps was Jewish;
ditto the girls in Butler, across the street. Jewlane, some called it.
I wasn't anti-Semitic as far as I knew, but then I hadn't known
a lot of Jews in Oklahoma, and hence their sudden abundance
in college seemed another feature of my overall alienation. At a
dorm party that first week I said as much to a couple of good
old boys from Memphis, Marlon and Andy, the "Starr brothers,"
who were actually first cousins and the only congenial people I'd
met so far: "I dunno," I said, when asked whether I'd checked out
the "talent" yet. "Seems all the girls here are *Jewish*." Marlon and
Andy looked at each other. "Well," said Marlon, "that's not really
a problem for Andy and me, since we're Jewish too." Mortified, I
spluttered some kind of idiotic disclaimer that I refuse to remember, such is my lingering trauma. And the following year—in
atonement, I like to think—I made a big stink among my Waspy
fraternity brothers, demanding we give a bid to Jim Gold from
Oklahoma City (one of Kelli's friends), who became my "little
brother" and later CEO of Bergdorf's.

In those days Tulane was almost 50 percent Greek, and lest
I become a Karate Clubber or Frisbee-tossing stoner, I pledged
Sigma Alpha Epsilon, the first fraternity founded in the South (on
the fertile banks of the Black Warrior River in Tuscaloosa). Dead
drunk, I was practically dragged to the house that first night of
rush by a girl with whom I'd made out at a riverboat party the
night before. She delivered me like a sack of soggy, redirected mail
and went on her way. Insofar as my eighteen-year-old self belonged
anywhere at Tulane, he belonged there—that is, he dearly *wished* to
belong with such supernormal specimens of the haute bourgeoisie:
a lot of boozy, ruddy-faced blokes from Choate, Woodberry Forest,
Lawrenceville, or their local country day, attired in oxford shirts

starched stiff as cardboard and pants of khaki or startling plaid, all their haircuts done, it seemed, by the same no-nonsense barber.

A few months later I moved to the SAE house, encountering Koenraad (in his karate togs) as I skittered down the steps at Phelps with my suitcase in hand. I'd told him nothing. "You are leaving?" he asked in his wistful way. I hadn't been a good roommate, much less a friend, but I was one of the very few people the poor guy knew. I clasped his hand feelingly and we parted forever.

FOR THE PAST year or so, Scott's public behavior had been almost exemplary: he was now a full-fledged waiter at the *best restaurant in town,* as Kelli would have it, he took classes at the Drahn School of Business (which prepared one for white-collar employment as a "data-entry specialist" or retail manager who could handle the books), and his Oldsmobile was still intact after several months in his care. Best of all, he continued to be a functioning, appreciative member of our new family: he was respectful toward Sandra, doting toward Kelli, and an eager playmate for Aaron—perhaps a bit too eager, as he broke the kid's glasses once by drilling him in the head with a football. But nobody expected perfection, and by the time Scott's twenty-first birthday came around my father was ready to make a large gesture, putting down the security deposit and first month's rent on a sleek one-bedroom unit in an apartment complex not far from Nichols Hills. I never got a chance to visit Scott there, but I was told about the chromium furniture and mirrored walls, the gatehouse and swimming pool and so on.

And that's not all. As my brother had proven himself a careful driver (my own views weren't canvassed), he also deserved a better car than the stalwart Oldsmobile that didn't even have a fucking *stereo*, he liked to point out. The car was Sandra's idea—she thought my brother needed some extra incentive, a vote of confidence at age twenty-one: he was a true adult now, and as long as he did his best ("whatever that may be") he should have nice, adult things. Since young men tend to identify with their cars to a morbid degree, this was deemed crucial to my brother's self-esteem—and what was the matter with Scott, really, if not low self-esteem? With Sandra and my father, then, he went shopping one day for a car.

"So what d'you think?" the friendly salesmen would ask him after a test drive.

And eerily Scott would remain silent. With a nervous laugh perhaps (exchanging a look with Burck and Sandra), the salesmen would repeat their question.

As if pained to oblige them even that much, Scott would jerk his head *No.*

"You want to try the same model in a different color?"

No.

"Something a little more compact maybe? Faster? Better mileage?"

No. No. No.

"So, um, maybe you'd prefer . . . ?"

"I'd *prefer* not to drive something that's an *obvious* piece of shit."

Truth be known, Scott was antagonized by salesmen, or anyone he suspected of tricking him or looking down on him in some way, however subtle. This included most people in service-related capacities—bartenders, store clerks, fellow waiters—and it got worse if Scott was in the company of family or someone he needed to impress. I can honestly say I was never in a particular kind of public situation with Scott when he didn't embarrass me with that weird hostility of his. On the other hand, he was the kindest of men toward bums, minorities, old people, children, pretty girls, and women of a certain age.

Sandra had never quite seen this side of Scott, and for that matter had never seen *anybody* use that sort of language around perfect strangers, and even my father's aplomb began to sag after a few hours.

"You know what?" Sandra told Burck that night. They were sitting on the patio coddling well-deserved cocktails; the long day of test drives had not borne fruit. "If anybody should get a new car, it's *you*."

And so they decided to give Scott my father's five-year-old Sedan de Ville, which after all was immaculate (except for a salvaged right-front wheel that only I knew about). My brother tried to be gracious but was vividly downcast, viewing the old boat as a booby prize, hardly better than his Oldsmobile. I think my father might have soothed his disappointment by installing a state-of-the-art stereo system. Scott had said hard things about the radios in those cars he'd test-driven.

A week or so later, when Scott was due for dinner, Burck and Sandra stood on their front lawn getting some air and letting the dog pee; suddenly they heard what sounded like a swiftly approaching typhoon. The grass hummed under their feet; the dog bolted back into the house. Just as they thought surely the world would explode, the storm gulped out and was punctuated by screeching tires—my brother's abrupt arrival at the curb. He'd been listening to a bit of music while driving around the streets of Nichols Hills as if on the Autobahn.

By then the car's title had been transferred, and besides, "Scott's an adult now!" as Sandra liked to say. There was nothing to do but wait. They didn't wait long. Almost a month to the day after he turned twenty-one, my brother reduced an entire 1976 Cadillac Sedan de Ville to scrap metal. The details were sketchy to the driver and hence to posterity. The car was found strewn around an entrance ramp to the Northwest Expressway—a trail of glittering detritus that led like Hansel and Gretel's breadcrumbs to a smoldering hull well beyond the guardrail. Scott had involved no other motorists in his accident; indeed the car seemed to have been driven by some mad ghost, since no charred or shockingly mutilated remains were found anywhere near the scene. That was another motif in my brother's career. No matter how bad the mishap, he generally emerged unscathed, an outcome my mother summed up with an old German adage, *Unkraut vergeht nicht*: "Weeds don't die!"

The only injuries Scott suffered that day came later—a few nasty abrasions that resulted from his smashing every bit of glass in his sleek new apartment. Scott would always insist that this was a sober, considered decision on his part.

"But Scott," I said later, during a candid chat, "almost every surface *in* the place was glass."

"That's what made it so tempting, Zwieb. Haven't you ever felt that way?"

I confessed I hadn't.

"Well," said Scott, slugging my shoulder a bit too hard, "maybe *you're* the one who's fucked up!"

So Scott left the scene of the accident and walked, in whatever condition, back to his apartment and smashed all the glass. The illusion of spaciousness would have collapsed once the mirrors were broken, and because he felt hemmed-in and guilty (I guess), Scott departed, walking a mile or two to my father's house. I like to imagine his progress through Nichols Hills, a kind of monitory apparition to the residents of that affluent banlieue. "An advocate," as Cheever wrote of one wretched, drunken protagonist, "for the lame, the diseased, the poor, for those who through no fault of their own live out their lives in misery and pain. To the happy and the wellborn and the rich he had this to say—that for all their affection, their comforts, and their privileges, they would not be spared the pangs of anger and lust and the agonies of death."

Kelli was alone at my father's house when Scott arrived. She was sitting in a big chair by the front window, doing her homework, when she sensed she was being watched, or maybe she heard something. In any event she turned around and saw Scott's face in the window. Kelli was too polite to scream at the sight of her own stepbrother; I imagine she even summoned a weak smile. Scott let himself in and sat at her feet. There was glass dust in his hair and tiny points of blood all over his face and scalp, but otherwise he seemed fine. He held Kelli's hand and petted her leg as he told her what he'd done that day. Finally Sandra and my father came home, and Scott seemed happy to see them.

BY THE TIME I came home for Christmas that year, everything was back to normal. Scott had found yet another apartment near Todd the Tortoise and was now adept at using public transportation. One day we sat at his little card table—placed with a certain geometric nicety vis-à-vis his other belongings—and after he'd discussed the Cadillac crash and its aftermath as if he were explaining some esoteric hobby, he went on to describe his daily routine. Each morning he awoke at five forty-five, showered, and ate cereal at his card table while watching Bullwinkle on a six-inch TV. Then he made a snack for later and walked five blocks to catch a bus that took him to the Drahn School of Business. His classes ended at ten thirty, and if he had to work a lunch shift at the restaurant there was a different bus to catch; otherwise he went home, ate, read (*Rolling Stone*, *Stereo Review*, or *Tiger Beat*) and napped until the dinner shift. A coworker took him home at night, when Scott would carry his little TV to bed and watch Carson until he fell asleep.

I asked him what sort of drugs he was doing these days, and Scott reared back and said "*Zwiiieeeeeeeeb*" in a tone of antic mock-reproach. The exchange was typical of our grown-up dynamic: that is, I tended to remark on the seedier side of his life with a kind of derisive sangfroid, as though he were incapable of shocking me further, and my brother would wax indignant in a way that was meant to rebuke my cynicism while implying that I was at least somewhat correct. We had a similar sense of humor.

But this time he insisted I was mistaken. When did he have time for recreational drugs? And where would he get the money? Certainly not from our father, who'd cut him off without a sou after that Cadillac business. Scott paid his own bills including his fees at Drahn, he said, showing me a couple of report cards as evidence of his new seriousness: straight A's. I imagine most of his fellow students were the kind of dim hicks who used to amuse Scott in high school, and probably he enjoyed the mild challenge of shining in their midst. But once the challenge was over—he got his diploma the following May—he never mentioned the place again and never to my knowledge sought employment relevant to the skills he'd acquired.

MEANWHILE THERE WERE inklings that all was not well, or not as well as Scott would have one think. That spring, while he was in the home stretch at Drahn, he was arrested on a charge of disturbing the peace. He'd been spotted dangling from a horizontal flagpole at the top of Fifty Penn Place—perhaps the tallest building in the northwest suburbs of Oklahoma City—the first three floors of which were occupied by posh shops and cafés. Quite a little crowd had gathered below, a lot of genteel lunching ladies, I imagine, an audience that would have pleased Scott.

In May my mother finished her bachelor's degree magna cum laude, a few days after I came home for summer vacation and Scott got his Drahn diploma. She particularly wanted the three of us, her ex-husband and two sons, to attend her graduation in Norman. It would be a nice little reunion, a way to acknowledge that things had turned out not-so-badly, what with Burck's happy marriage, Marlies's degree, and Scott's slow but steady progress in the world (despite the odd misadventure). As for me, well, I'd made it through my first year at Tulane with middling grades, but that was about the best anyone seemed to expect at that point.

The plan was to pick up Scott at his apartment in the Earl Hotel—his last sleazy apartment, we hoped, now that Drahn would surely land him at least among the lower rungs of the middle class. He didn't answer the door, so my father and I let ourselves in. A number of things were wrong. Scott was lying on a ratty sofa, eyes and mouth smiling as if in greeting. He was wearing his old vagrant uniform of checked trousers (gone in the crotch) and yellowed T-shirt. He looked at us and laughed, and for a moment I had a sense of being ludicrously overdressed; that was the year I affected bow ties and madras trousers.

Then Scott began to talk: his phrases, or riffs perhaps, had all the cadence of normal speech, but not a single word was intelligible as English (or German). He went on and on, pausing to laugh from time to time. He remained recumbent.

My father considered him there on the sofa. "Son?"

Scott gave him a wavering look, sort of rocking his body from side to side. He was talking the whole time.

"*Son?*" My father patted his cheek as if to wake him.

"He's not asleep," I said.

"Hm." My father sat on the edge of the sofa and stroked Scott's hair a moment, staring into that beatific face of his. Scott's speech had become a kind of happy crooning. Finally my father rose and walked out the door without a word. I followed, shutting the door behind me. The crooning pursued us down the hall.

The following Monday, Scott called my father at his office and asked why we hadn't picked him up the other day as planned. Burck ventured to explain.

"I was sleeping!" said Scott. "You should've woken me up!"

"We tried. Your eyes were open the whole time."

"I was *sleeping*," he insisted, and went on about how disappointed he'd been when he realized he'd missed Mom's graduation, etc. He even became tearful about it, and my father ended up apologizing.

THAT SUMMER BURCK and Sandra went abroad for a month or so. They'd arranged to pick up a BMW right off the assembly line in Germany, whence they planned to drive it around Europe before putting it on a boat to the States. In the meantime a few family friends were supposed to check on Kelli and me, though I don't think anyone was very diligent about it. We were old enough to care for ourselves, while little Aaron was away in Dallas with his father.

We'd moved to a new house in Nichols Hills with a pool, and most of my weekend time was divided between swimming, reading, and tippling, while Kelli was off with her boyfriend for the most part. I enjoyed myself. I liked being alone, but I also liked having friends over to share my happiness; that summer was perhaps the closest I ever came to achieving a golden mean in this respect. It made me feel benevolent.

One day I was entertaining five or six friends when my brother called. He had tickets for the Cheap Trick concert that night and wondered if I wanted to come. This was a novel invitation and rather touching, though I wasn't interested for any number of reasons; still, I wanted to make some sort of reciprocal gesture. I explained that I was busy that night (true), then asked if he'd like to come over and spend the day with me and my friends. It was the first time I'd ever willingly exposed others to the adult Scott, who seemed moved by the offer.

He rode over on a motorcycle he'd recently bought cheap from one of his coworkers. Full of my own benevolence, I pretended not to mind that he was drinking a beer as he rode up, sans helmet and license to operate a motorcycle or any other motorized vehicle. I looked at his eyes, assessed the slur in his voice, and figured he'd taken maybe a bong hit and drunk three or four beers. It could have been worse, and besides he seemed so happy to see me, just to be there, that I couldn't bring myself to remark on the fact that he was half in the bag by noon and should be more careful, at least around my friends.

Everybody tried to be nice to Scott. They knew he had problems and knew, too, that there was something momentous about his being here at the pool—this brother whose existence I rarely acknowledged. My friends acted as if they'd been enlisted in a secret charity, as I suppose they had. Scott sat on the edge of the shallow end, near the gazebo and beer, while, one by one, my friends swam over to chat with him. After a few hours I began to relax a little—even to cast ahead to other such occasions, to plan a whole summer project of easing my brother into the social mainstream and presenting him, at last, to my proud father.

I was in the kitchen when I caught a glimpse of Scott lurching toward the bathroom. He caromed off a wall and splashed beer all over the floor, righting himself like a fullback pawing his way into the end zone with a scrappy bit of second effort. I dropped what I was doing and waited outside the bathroom. He was in there a long time, then burst out the door and collided with me full speed.

I got back on my feet and glared at him there on the floor. He was laughing and wanted me to laugh with him.

"What've you been taking?" I asked.

Scott looked hurt. "Whaddya *mean*? Justa few beers!" His head wobbled with denial.

"You are so full of shit."

"Justa few *beers* . . ."

I went outside and asked my friends to leave—all but sweet-natured, redheaded Matt, my old pot-smoking companion, who came closest to being a confidant where drugs and my brother were concerned. Matt wanted to tell me something in private. The others didn't have to ask what was wrong, as they'd already noticed (while I was gloating over my benevolence) that something odd was happening to Scott.

We were all standing around the driveway saying sheepish good-byes when one friend pointed to the roof and laughed. I looked. Scott had somehow clambered up there with Aaron's banana-seat bicycle, which he was now poised (if that's the word) to ride into the pool for our entertainment.

"You think that's *funny*?" I said to my friends, all of whom had succumbed to a kind of sickly mirth—these people whose parents had never divorced and whose siblings were a lot of regular guys and gals just like themselves. "Get the hell outta here!" I started herding them into their cars, giving one of them an extra push when he paused to glance back at my brother, who'd apparently sensed he was losing his audience and rolled off the roof without further ado.

He wasn't badly hurt. Ours was a largeish one-story house whose eaves were maybe eight feet off the ground. I found the little bicycle crumpled at the edge of the pool, its front wheel wanly spinning, while my brother sputtered "Fuck, my knee!" (laughing) and splashed around a bit before losing his balance and slipping underwater.

"*What're you, fucking six years old?*" I yelled, when he came to the surface again. "What've you been taking?"

"Justa few *beers*..." Plaintive.

My friend Matt waved me inside. He seemed reluctant to speak. For maybe five minutes we just stood at the sliding door watching my brother, who was trying to mount a Styrofoam raft with a singular lack of success. Twenty or so times he jumped on belly-first, only to slip off the side or capsize, hugging the thing for dear life; then he tried hiking a leg over, both legs, both sides, many times ... Plainly Scott lacked the coordination to board that raft—he fell fifty times, a hundred, it wasn't going to happen—but he seemed to find meaning in the effort per se. The raft was his thing. At some point I changed clothes and rejoined Matt at the sliding door. Scott was still at it. He reminded me of a trick-riding clown I'd seen at the Vinita rodeo.

Finally Matt spoke: Scott, he said, had been shooting heroin in the bathroom. How did Matt know? Well, because Scott had offered him some.

"And what did you say?" I asked.

"I said no. I told him thanks, but no."

"And what did he say?"

"He told me not to worry about needles. He said he'd, you know, do it for me."

I thanked Matt and asked him to leave. Then I went outside and sat on a chaise longue by the pool. Scott had towed the raft to some steps in the shallow end, where he hoped to mount it in a sitting position; he stood on the top step and eyed that slab of Styrofoam as if it were a stabled bull.

"Having trouble?" I asked.

He spotted me there on the patio and broke into an ecstatic grin. We might have just encountered each other on the streets of a foreign city: What a surprise! Wie geht's, old man? . . .

"So now you're a junkie too?"

The smile wavered as he parsed this; then he looked plaintive again. "Whassa matter?" He looked at me with infinite self-pity: Why did I have to ruin everything? If he was happy, why couldn't I be happy too?

I went inside and phoned our mother. I explained the situation. At first she didn't believe me about the heroin, but when I told her what Matt had said (she knew Matt) and reminded her of what Burck and I had seen that day at the Earl Hotel, she believed it. She advised me to keep him there. I said it wouldn't be easy. I told her about the motorcycle and the Cheap Trick concert; moreover I had a dinner engagement with an old family friend, the fat chef/magician at the Grand Boulevard Restaurant, Scott's former employer.

"Well, cancel it!" said my mother.

I said he'd be here any minute, that he'd made a reservation at an excellent restaurant, and really I had no intention of missing a good meal for the sake of some junkie asshole who shoots up around my friends. I said as much while glaring directly into the misty eyes of the junkie in question, who'd tottered into the doorway with a look of dim foreboding. He stood there in his wet underwear, dripping on the floor.

"Whosa?" he asked.

"It's our mother," I said. "You want to talk to her?"

I held out the phone, which squawked "*Scott? Goddamn it! What've you been . . .*"

A number of complicated attitudes seemed to play on Scott's face: there was the haunted look of a little boy caught; there was jaded impatience with Marlies's browbeating; there was not a little humor. All this blended at last into a look of nonchalant denial. He shook his head at the phone with a bleary frown, then on second thought muttered "Justa few *beers*" and fell back against the dining-room table, folding his arms as if his staggering were natural.

"Well, there you have it," I said.

"Keep him there," said my mother. "And call me back."

I hung up and asked Scott to give me the keys to his motorcycle. He looked stricken, amused, incredulous: *Why?*

"You know why. Don't give me that shit. Matt told me all about it. Give me the fucking keys!"

He shook his head.

"Scott," I said, "listen carefully. You're in no condition to ride a motorcycle. You can hardly stand up. Feel free to spend the night here, but you're not going to any goddamn Cheap Trick concert."

"Justa few *beers*" was the best he could muster—or rather he couldn't be bothered: that inane little mantra was good enough, it seemed, for the likes of me. He stood there with his arms folded, weaving slightly, mouth agape with infantile defiance.

At this point I snapped and did something violent, resulting in a softball-sized hole in the expensive, upholstered wallpaper Sandra had picked out in the course of redecorating the dining room. They had to cover this hole with a picture for some months. I simply can't remember how I did it. Did I throw something? Did I use my fist? Such was the extremity of that moment—such was my blinding rage toward the vacuous, fucked-up face of my incorrigibly fucked-up brother—that I lapsed into a kind of fugue state.

But I was instantly sobered by the hole in the wall, as well as by the sound of knocking on the door. Chef had arrived.

"Hold on!" I yelled. I looked at Scott. He was pondering the hole and looking vaguely hurt about things, as though he'd been spanked on his birthday.

"Scott," I said, "promise me you won't go to that concert tonight."

He sniveled that the tickets had cost him twenty *bucks*, that he'd been looking forward to it for *months*, and (it went without saying) he had so little to look forward to. I handed over the thirteen or so dollars in my wallet; if he promised to stay home, I said, I'd give him the seven later. Did he promise?

After a pause (*knock knock knock*), he nodded. I patted his shoulder and started to go.

"You're leaving . . . ?"

"Yep."

Scott wagged his head. That was not part of the deal as he saw it.

"Who're you . . . ?"

"Chef."

He took a deep breath. "Fat—fuck. No talent . . . faggot."

"Scott, I'll see you later," I said. "Get some sleep."

" . . . Can I come?"

"*No.*"

At the door I squeezed past our friend Chef.

"What's the hurry, you little shit?" he said, then turned around and faced Scott there in the doorway. They hadn't seen each other in years, not since the man had finally fired Scott. My brother stood glaring in a way that was meant to be menacing, but most of his strength was spent on the mere standing, so that he couldn't quite focus his menace. He was still there, and still glaring, when we pulled out of the driveway.

"God," Chef sighed a block or so later. He shook his head, his breath whistling in his beard. "God, I wish I hadn't seen that."

During dinner I remembered to call Marlies back. I excused myself and found a pay phone.

"Where are you?" she asked.

I told her.

"You left Scott alone?" This in a neutral voice my mother used when she was beyond vexation.

"What else could I do? He wouldn't give me his keys."

She sighed. "You know where he is now?"

"He's not at the house?"

"He's in jail."

And then she proceeded to explain what I surely already knew—had known, indeed, when I left my brother alone at the door: namely, that he had promptly endeavored to ride his motor-cycle to the Cheap Trick concert, and had naturally been arrested for driving while intoxicated, without a license, and whatever else. I remember being impressed that he'd almost made it all the way to the Myriad Convention Center downtown, where the concert took place. Another block or so and all might have been well—in which case, no doubt, he would have reprised the "Justa few *beers*" mantra for my benefit.

———

BECAUSE OF PRIOR drug-related offenses, Scott was sentenced to a state rehab facility in Norman, a grimly generic redbrick asylum called Griffin Memorial. My father visited him in August (after he and Sandra returned from Europe) and later mailed me a photo Sandra had taken: there was Burck in a summer suit and Panama hat, a rather formal hand on his son's shoulder, the latter looking very institutional with his buzz cut and scowl.

I'd been back at college for a couple of weeks when my father phoned to say, in a tired voice, that Scott was hopeless.

The night before, he and Sandra and Marlies had attended their first and only family session at the rehab facility. There were many families at these sessions, many patients, and the process went something like this: patients were each given a chance to speak without interruption, the idea being that they should confront their parents about particular things the parents had done to contribute to their children's maladjustment; then the parents were given a chance to respond, again without interruption. Finally the floor was thrown open to general feedback. At all times one was enjoined to be as "objective" as possible, while avoiding any hint of opprobrious language: "It makes me sad when you call me 'worthless' . . ."

According to three out of four witnesses to whom I was privy, my brother was easily the most obnoxious patient, the most bitter and self-absorbed and serenely immune to contradiction of any kind. Sobriety did not agree with him. He pointed out that all his doctors were assholes and oafs, ditto his fellow patients (who hated his guts); the only people in the place whom he exempted were a few orderlies and janitors.

As for his family, well, when Scott got to that part, he fixed a baleful look on my father, mother, and Sandra in turn, then in a calm "objective" voice (his satirical concession to the prevailing etiquette) recited his grievances—to wit, that he'd been persecuted on a routine basis almost from infancy. He went on at some length about this.

While my brother spoke, a number of patients violated protocol with catcalls of *motherfucker* and *boohoo!* and *kiss my ass*. When it was over they erupted with a roar of hatred that lingered almost a full minute. At first Scott winced a little, then he smirked.

Burck sat there staring at him. Finally, after the insults had subsided into a fraught silence, he took a deep breath and spoke:

"I don't know who you are."

Scott shifted comfortably in his chair and waited for the rest, but abruptly my father put his hat back on and walked out. Sandra and Marlies looked at each other and followed.

Scott caught up with them in the parking lot, trotting alongside, in front, around them, yelling, "*Where the fuck're you going? I'm your son, goddammit! I'm your son!*" At some point he grabbed my mother's coat sleeve—or *yanked her around by the arm*, depending on who tells it—demanding that she, at least, stay.

"And I'll never forgive myself," my father told me over the phone, "but then I hit him."

If indeed my brother had gotten in their faces and hollered abuse, if indeed he'd violently accosted my mother, then of course he deserved whatever he got. But Scott would always insist that he'd simply grabbed our mother's sleeve and tried to hang on, that he couldn't believe that they (she in particular) would simply turn their backs on him, *leave* him in such a place—perhaps forever, or so it seemed at the time—and he further insisted that he'd simply lost heart when our father had punched him in the face "for no reason." But Sandra claims that Scott actually shoved Burck and was ready to fight; with a kind of bashful pride, she tells of how she jumped on Scott's back and pummeled him over the head with a heavy coin-filled purse until he backed off, staggering, and they were able to complete their getaway.

"He's hopeless," my father sighed.

"Absolutely," I said. After a pause I saw fit to add, "Your only regret should be that you didn't come to that conclusion *years* ago."

"I don't know . . . sometimes—" But he didn't finish. "So how're your classes? You *are* taking classes, I hope."

I WAS TAKING classes, but mostly I was immersed in the inanity of fraternity life. I'd returned early that fall for rush week, and my days were a pleasant round of beery, earnest meetings and parties into the night. One of my two roommates was a guy named Jay whose family owned Pontchartrain Beach amusement park; since we hadn't found an apartment yet, the three of us lived that first month in the Lakeview home of Jay's parents, almost a half-hour drive from campus. I ruined a couple of neckties by passing out on their wet lawn—this after somehow driving back from whatever wingding had transpired the night before. One morning I was woken there on the grass by the family retainer, a crabby old black woman named Oralea, who prodded me with her foot; when she saw I was awake, she hobbled back into the house without a word. Breakfast was waiting.

It was after a particularly festive day that my father called and told me that Family Night at the rehab center had gone poorly. My roommates and I had just found an Uptown duplex apartment, and that morning we'd driven golf carts around the amusement park after loading up cases of free liquor from the Bali Hai Club, where patrons went to soak while their kiddies rode rides;

the liquor filled an entire closet in our new apartment. Later we went back to Jay's house in Lakeview and laughed away the afternoon playing pool, drinking, and listening to Jay's jukebox. Then the phone rang and, after a bit of cordial banter, Jay mouthed "your dad" and handed it over. Burck asked how I was doing, and seemed to have all the time in the world to listen while I gave him a somewhat expurgated account of my days.

By the end of that school year, our duplex apartment had come to resemble the den of latchkey urchins whose guardians have fled for good. Jay could always provide fresh glasses from the Bali Hai Club, and we'd simply grab a clean one out of a new box as needed and leave the dirty ones, hundreds of them, to grow into furry little skylines of mold along every counter. The garbage was nudged out the door maybe once a month, and during the last couple of weeks it got so bad that I hated to leave my bedroom, lest I spot the gray blur of a startled mouse in the hall. I learned the extent to which life can become weirdly habitual. After final exams, we went to the Bahamas with a fraternity brother whose family kept a condo on Windermere Island; after a week of card-playing, gin-drinking boredom, of flaccid male nakedness on a sun-splashed terrace, we flew back to Miami and drove twenty hours to that forsaken duplex, whose open door released a miasma that put one in mind of a mass grave. And yet it must have smelled similar the week before, if only we'd had the faculties to notice. Then on my way back to Oklahoma—a journey I began as quickly as I could gather my tainted things—I was stopped for speeding in Denton, Texas, and jailed when it was discovered that my car was actually owned by one Gayle Mackenroth, who proved to be Jay's grandmother; he and I had swapped vehicles one day on a drunken whim without bothering to transfer titles. And finally, while waiting to explain all this to a judge, my hands began to swell and turn a kind of blotchy magenta. In despair by then, I assumed this was syphilis or dropsy or some other manifestation of a Dorian Gray–like moral rot. It was, in fact, the result of too much sun.

WHEN SCOTT GOT out of rehab that fall, my father decided to give him another chance, this time on the condition that he see a psychiatrist of Burck's choosing. Scott consented. The psychiatrist was a man of some local renown, a family friend named Dr. Hauber, a pudgy-faced Frans Hals figure who used to have giggly chats in German with my mother.

Dr. Hauber told my father that Scott was under the impression he'd been cruelly beaten as a child. Burck, I suppose, endeavored to disabuse the man, and ultimately Hauber declared—wrongly, I think—that Scott was a paranoid schizophrenic. Dr. Hauber's verdict, along with certain other events, helped validate my father's previous opinion that Scott was hopeless, and by the following summer he was back in the outer darkness again.

"When a child is young," Burck explained one night (perhaps he was relating Hauber's analogy), "you can catch him if he falls. Then he gets a little older and falls from a higher place. Maybe you can still catch him. But finally he's a full-grown adult and falls off the top of a building—then you have to decide: either get out of the way or be crushed."

I thought of Scott dangling from that flagpole at the top of Fifty Penn Place, and no wonder he seemed unimpressed by my own madcappery. For him there was no Bali Hai Club, no larky sojourns on Windermere Island. Though his apartment was tidier than mine, Scott's life belonged to a different, far grimmer plane of reality, as I was reminded during a summer lunch at that restaurant where he still worked, though demoted to busboy. It was our first meeting in almost a year; Marlies had insisted I see Scott and pave the way, if possible, to reconciliation between him and Burck. Also I confess to a certain morbid curiosity.

Something about the waiter's manner, when he told me Scott was in the downstairs dining room, let me know I was in for a bad time; the man seemed pained by a stomachache he didn't care to discuss. "Scott—" he began, then grimaced and pointed downstairs. He disappeared into the kitchen. I went downstairs. I was halfway there when I spotted Scott from the landing. He was sitting at a corner table, writing a letter with an emphatic, wounded look, his face flushed with beer and what appeared to be incipient tears. I considered bolting, but finally went over and said hello.

He didn't look up. He kept writing until he came to a stop, then capped his gold-plated fountain pen—a gift from Burck when Scott had graduated from Drahn—and put the letter aside.

"Who're you writing?"

"Ma," he said. "I was just telling her that if you didn't show up—"

"Why wouldn't I show up?"

"You're late."

I looked at my watch. "Five minutes?"

"We said noon."

"No, Scott, I'm pretty sure we said twelve thirty."

"Noon."

For a moment I thought he'd pursue the matter, nastily, but he just sat there shaking his head and looking depressed. With two fingers he picked up his bottle and waggled it at a passing waiter, who asked, "This your brother, Scott?"

He nodded. I ordered a beer too, and the waiter went away.

"So tell me about yourself," Scott sighed.

I tried, doing my best to stress the sordid aspects of my life—

the drunken blackouts, the verminous duplex, the mossy glasses, the jail in Denton, and so on, but my brother didn't cheer up or laugh because it wasn't funny. The fact remained that I was a student at a decent college (as my mother was keen to remind Scott), having the time of my life, and doubtless I struck my brother as the kind of simpering twit who finds his own life *so* amusing, all the more so in light of his (that is, my) basic contentment. However, another topic of conversation (*Mom tells me you're a busboy again; how'd that happen?*) was slow to recommend itself, so I kept prattling until Scott interrupted.

"How's Pa?"

I said our father seemed fine. "In fact," I added, "never better."

"How so?"

"Oh, you know, just in good fettle. Fewer worries, I guess."

My brother abruptly reared in his seat, raking his eyes over the room until they fell on our waiter. "How're those *beers* coming, Phil?"

The waiter paused with a laden tray. "In a moment, big guy," he said, with a faint edge to his voice, that of a waiter addressing a busboy. My brother kept his eye on the man until he was certain some positive action was being taken; then he turned back to me.

"Well, isn't that nice?" he said.

"Isn't what nice?"

"That Pa's so cheerful. That he's so—so peachy-keen."

"Yes," I said, "it certainly is."

We sat there glaring at each other. The beers arrived.

"Will you guys be ordering?" the waiter asked. He clapped his hands, once, twice, at his waist. "Or d'you need a few minutes?" Clap. "Or—"

"We need a few minutes," my brother said flatly. The man departed with a worried glance over his shoulder.

"What's good here?" I asked Scott.

"Nothing. Order a hamburger. So does he ever mention me?"

"Papa? Not much . . . or no, wait, come to think of it, I seem to recall something he said about how you like to tell people you were beaten as a child."

There was a pause. A vague look of shame, or something, fluttered around Scott's face like a skittish bird, then flew away. "He told you that?"

"Yes."

"And what, he denied it?"

"It's not a question of denying it, Scott. He knows what happened. I know what happened. You were *spanked* a few times. If you want to blame your whole fucked-up life on that, fine, but don't—"

"When I was a little boy," he said, loading the words with poignancy, "he'd make me drop my pants and lie on the bed. Then he'd take off his belt and start lashing the bed with it, just to scare me. When I was four or five years old . . ."

He went on like that, building to the climax of the actual spanking (or "beating" or "lashing"). His eyes peered at some vision over my left shoulder. I didn't bother to interrupt.

"Bravo," I said when he'd finished, limply clapping my hands.

Scott swallowed and gave a quick angry laugh. "You better watch your ass, Zwieb."

"Or what?"

He gave me a look of loony menace, as in *You'll see.*

"*Fuck you*," I said. "Listen: I have the same father and I got the same spankings. The *reason* he whipped the bed was because half the time he had no intention of whipping *us*, and it sure as hell didn't traumatize *me*. So fuck you if you can't take a joke. How *dare* you. You practically ruin the man's *life*—"

"Oh yeah, his life is so—"

"You ruin *both* our parents' lives, and now you—"

Our waiter was back. "Guys, guys," he said, frantically patting the air, "keep it down or you're gonna have to—"

"Tell *him* to be quiet," said Scott with elaborate calm. He crossed his legs and shrugged. "He just went apeshit on me."

"Okay, Scott. Just—" The waiter shook his head and walked away.

Scott watched him go, then leaned as far across the table as possible without leaving his seat. "You better not get me fired, man," he said.

I sat there looking at him, my eyelids drooping, as if to suggest that getting fired from his little busboy job was about the best thing that could happen to him, short of dropping dead. I didn't trust myself to speak.

Appearing to calm down for both of us, Scott crossed his legs again and leaned back, steepling his fingers; then he remarked in a measured tone that I'd never really "gotten" our father. "He's the Wizard of Oz," said Scott. "You know?"

"No," I said. "I don't know. Tell me."

"Smoke and mirrors, Zwieb. The whole *persona*. The great man in public, you know, the whole *facade* of wisdom and benevolence. But underneath the whole—the whole illusion—"

"You mutt," I said. "You're a mutt." *Mutt?* I don't know why the word occurred to me, but at any rate I let it sink in. "Mutt. Tell you what, mutt, unless you apologize for everything you've said about our father today, I'm leaving."

My brother said nothing.

"So long, mutt."

I was halfway up the stairs when I heard a mumbled "Sorry." I paused to look down at my brother: he was glaring at the table as though in furious pain, as though the word "sorry" had been gouged out of him with a toothpick. I kept going. I was out the door and striding into the parking lot when I heard a rush of footfalls—too late. The impact caused my last swallow of beer to gush out of my stomach; then I was on the asphalt with a sour taste in my mouth.

Above me I heard a rapid whisper: "Sorry, Zwieb, I just . . ."

"Get away from me."

I stumbled in the direction of my car. At first Scott plucked at me from behind—my elbow, a belt loop, a pocket—saying "please" a lot, and "Zwieb," but when I kept going he grabbed my shirt collar and yanked. I fell backward out of my polo shirt and landed on the pavement again, absurdly barebacked. I groped for my shirt, but Scott held it out of my reach.

"You can have it when you—"

"Keep it."

I got to my feet and resumed walking to my car with what I hoped was a kind of dignity, despite my skinny, scuffed-up bare torso. I was conscious of a huddle of witnesses gathering around the exit. For their benefit, no doubt, Scott hugged me almost gently from behind and planted his feet.

"Zwieb, *stop*. Goddamn it . . ."

I waited for him to let go; finally he released me from the bear hug but kept hold of my wrist, deftly transferring my wadded shirt to his left hand as he did so. Once I had an arm free I gave him a glancing blow to the forehead. He glared at me, blinking, but held on. I punched him in the mouth and flailed wildly out of his grasp. He caught up with me a few feet from my car and tackled me to the pavement again. This time he stayed on top and didn't speak when I told him to get off. I began to yell for help. All my brother's strength went into holding me there; every few moments he'd let out a wet little pant or a snuffle.

"Let him up, Scott."

"C'mon man, you can't *do* this shit here . . ."

Two big guys in aprons were peeling him off me; our waiter looked on. All three spoke to Scott in low, soothing voices, as if to a hurting child.

"Just cool it, man. It's over. Calm down now."

"You okay?" one of them asked me.

On his feet again, my brother was bouncing on his toes with a pathetic swagger. He was trying not to cry, but his nasal voice had a quaver. "I didn't *do* anything to him, Phil," he told our waiter. "You saw! I was just sitting there *talking* to him, man, and he starts—"

Phil the waiter was shaking his head and patting the air. "You don't have to explain to *me*, Scott. This is between you and your brother. I just think—"

"Then he gets up and just *leaves* me there—"

Scott's voice broke and he buried his face in his hands. One of the big guys put an arm around him and gave him a consoling jostle. All three were glancing at me with a curious mixture of sympathy and reproach.

"He needs to get out of here *now*," the waiter told me, "before the manager comes out. Can you give him a ride?"

I sighed, said sure, and picked my shirt off the pavement where Scott had dropped it. It was ripped at the collar and drooped loosely around my neck, exposing one nipple. My brother wouldn't uncover his face, so I touched his arm and guided him around to the passenger side of my car. The others were saying "Later, Scott" and "See you tomorrow, man," in kind voices, waving, before hurrying back to the restaurant.

Inside the car, my brother gathered his breath with a long sizzling hiss and held it, grimacing, then all at once doubled over sobbing. I drove. I couldn't bear it. Even now I can't bear it—the immensity of those minutes.

At some point I ventured to touch the back of his neck and ask where he lived. He confided the usual terrible address. I parked in an alley behind the place—the worst place yet—and we sat in silence, punctuated by his sniffles. Finally I asked if he was going to be all right.

"I don't know," he said in a hollow whisper. "I don't know, Zwieb." He sat there. Sometimes he'd let out a deep sigh, an exhausted *whew*. "You want to come up?" he asked finally, staring out the window.

"I'd like to," I said, "but I can't. I just don't have time. Sorry."

Scott seemed to accept the lie without bitterness, as if he were grateful I'd spared him the truth—namely that every second in his company was misery.

"Mind if I just sit here another minute?"

"Of course not."

He looked too tired to cry, but every few seconds the tears would come anyway and he'd grimace with an effort to hold them back. He coughed a number of times and said, "Do you think Papa—" He coughed again. "Do you think Papa will ever want to see me again?"

I decided to be honest. I said something to this effect: Our father would always forgive him in the end, and that was a pity, because it spared Scott the effort of *earning* his forgiveness. I told Scott that his life was repulsive ("sorry, but there it is"), that he'd brought nothing but heartache to anyone who'd ever made the mistake of caring for him. I told him that if he couldn't change he should just keep away. From all of us.

Somewhere in there Scott began to sob again. He spoke in mournful heaves, barely able to catch his breath: "How can you s-*say* that? . . . I'm your *brother*, Zwieb. I luh-*love* you. I'm your fucking *brother*..."

I stared out the window at the dreary littered lawns, the rusted monkey bars and scattered backyard crap of that awful neighborhood. All the while my brother was forcing words through his sobs:

"*Look* at me . . . my only friends are n-*niggers* . . . I can barely pay my shit—my shitty *rent*... I'm a fuck—fucking twenty-three-year-old b-*bus*boy . . . I can't get rid of these fucking *pimples*..."

I was about to say, as gently as possible, "Scott, whose fault is that?"—when he mentioned the pimples, something I could hardly blame him for. Finally I sighed and said I was sorry, but I had to go. I said I'd call him.

Scott nodded wearily, dragging a hand over his face. A string of snot stuck to his palm and he flung it out the window. "Promise?" he said.

"Promise."

It was the last I saw of him for a long time.

part III

a functioning
mediocrity

After she married my father, Sandra had given up her PR business at Burck's request, and now busied herself, frantically, with home improvement on a Utopian scale. My own bedroom in the new house was mine for two weeks or so toward the end of that first summer; when I returned for the holidays during my freshman year of college, every trace of my occupancy had been erased—crammed into the attic or thrown away outright—as the room was converted into the master suite and I was consigned to guest quarters, which had the nicely appointed anonymity of a comfortable hotel. "Look what we did with *your* room!" said Sandra, meaning the guest room, as if I should thank her for such handsome accommodations (as I did), and my crappy belongings be damned.

An added feature in "my" new bedroom was certainly a plus: a sliding door that opened directly on to the back patio and swimming pool, so I could come and go without calling much attention to myself. This increased my sense of being a lodger as opposed to a family member, and I figured I might as well be a coddled lodger. My sybaritic weekend transit from bedroom to pool and back again, that summer after my freshman year, might have caused a strain if Sandra hadn't left for Europe in the nick of time. The second summer it did cause a strain—especially since I'd decided to go without a job for the first summer since age thirteen. Sandra is not a lazy woman; indeed she must stay busy at all times lest something inside her tighten and tighten and *snap* with an all but audible twang. When I returned from the Bahamas (by way of Denton, where I'd explained the car-title discrepancy to the judge and was let off with a modest fine), Sandra was engaged more than ever in turning her—their—at any rate not *my*—home into a gorgeous but practical retreat from the cares of the world, which entailed her scampering around in shorts giving decorous orders to laborers building fences and landscaping gardens and improving the gazebo and God knows what else. She might have been entirely happy in this, were it not for a certain lone figure in the pool. Watching me there—as she did at longer and more baneful intervals—she would thin her lips and knit her brow, as if I were masturbating instead of reading. The first few times our eyes met I tried smiling benignly, or giving her a little wave, and one day she didn't smile or wave back. A bad sign, given her usual civility.

One day she brightly approached me there in the pool. "Blake? Could you come here a minute?"

She had a job for me. There was a little sward on the side of the house where Sandra envisaged a brick path. Would I mind building it?—in other words (understood but naturally unspoken):

Would I mind getting off my dead ass for once and making a little contribution around here?

Why, not at all! *In two days* I accomplished the following: filled the bed of a pickup truck with sufficient bricks and concrete to build a twenty-foot brick path as specified, lugged the lot of it around to the side of the house, dug a uniform curving brick-deep ditch (marked off with sticks and string) where indicated, mixed the concrete, laid a three-foot-long pattern of bricks, and presented my work for inspection to Sandra, who (rightly) found it a ghastly botch and advised me to start over with sand rather than concrete; on the second day, then, I broke up the bricks with a sledgehammer, bought many bags of sand (and more bricks), lugged them to the worksite, and started over in a similar, but *much* neater, sand-based pattern. Sandra liked it. Indeed, she was quite pleasantly startled—or rather (human nature being what it is) a bit nettled, perhaps, to find her worst expectations so lavishly disappointed.

But I soon endeavored to make it up to her. For a couple of days I continued work on the path, but less and less, laying a few more feet of bricks that third day, maybe a foot or so the fourth, and finally letting day after day pass without so much as a glance in its direction. It was only July, after all: what was the hurry? I had the summer before me. If I'd continued to work at my initial speed, I would have finished in a week, tops, whereupon Sandra would have doubtless found some other project to keep me occupied and out of her pool, where I seemed determined to languish as a kind of Hogarthian portrait of indolence . . . though I didn't see it that way. On the contrary! I on my raft, reading a book, was nothing less than an Epicurean ideal—a well-contented mind and body—and it wasn't *my* fault that Sandra needed to be so *busy busy busy* every single waking moment.

Was it a matter of conscious rebellion on my part? I doubt it. Probably I was just lazy and self-involved and didn't really see the effect I was having on Sandra, or at any rate thought that if she had a problem with a young man attending to an ambitious reading/tanning program during his summer vacation, well, she needed to get over it. But Sandra took the situation *very* hard, and our relations never quite recovered. One day in mid-August or so, I was sitting in a breakfast nook whose window fronted my abortive brick path, when I noticed Sandra directing her main factotum, an affable Brit named Ivor, to finish the damn thing already. (Ivor had worked at the Oklahoma City Zoo when I was a kid, and he and Marlies were chums; because she loved animals he'd occasionally given her prairie dogs, chinchillas, sparrow hawks, and the like. He was a small pot-bellied man with a ruddy bearded face that hardly ever frowned. Sandra had appropriated him after he was downsized at the zoo and my mother moved away to Norman.) I hurried outside in my bathrobe.

"Wait wait wait—! What's this?"

"What do you *think*, Blake?" Sandra stood there with her arms tightly folded. She looked at me with a kind of vague, wondering, thin-lipped smile—perhaps her most hostile expression. "How long were you planning to leave this *ditch* in my yard?"

I pointed out that the summer wasn't over yet, and she told me that either I finish the path—*today*—or Ivor would. The latter stood crouching over the path, hanging fire, sheepishly turning a brick over and over in his hands.

I took the brick out of Ivor's hands and got to work, and I suppose three or four hours later I was done. Just like that. And it looked nice, too; it's there to this day. But of course it was too late for that to matter, and I couldn't help feeling a little rueful about how easy it would have been just to finish the job in a timely manner and remain in Sandra's good graces. But part of me, plainly, didn't want that. Part of me was taking a stand. The principle in question went something like this: she could purge me from the family by removing most evidence of my existence from her house, but she could not persuade me that there was anything inherently wrong about spending my summer reading in a pool.

From that day forward, whatever her niceness otherwise, Sandra said terrible things behind my back to whosoever would listen—her children, friends, neighbors, Burck's law partners, even our longtime maid, Katherine Jones, who doted on me and couldn't understand why I was determined to cross a nice person like Sandra, who in her best Lady Bountiful fashion had taken her to see *The Color Purple*. Quite simply I combined everything Sandra disliked in a human being, and was a rival for her husband's affection besides.

Many years later, I observed Sandra at an engagement party for her daughter. She'd run into one of Kelli's old flames, an amiable jock named Don, who'd gone to fat but was still handsome, still the sort of regular guy who means what he says and says what he means. With him, I noticed, Sandra was perfectly at ease. She laid a hand on his shoulder and they sat chatting for a long time; the change in Sandra was like Amanda Wingfield's at the end of *The Glass Menagerie*: "Now that we cannot hear [her] speech," the stage directions read, "her silliness is gone and she has dignity and tragic beauty." Watching Sandra with Don, I was sorry I'd been such a disappointment to her; toward them both, indeed, I felt something of Tonio Kröger's secret love for the "blond and blue-eyed, the fair and living, the happy, lovely, and commonplace," and I realized too that I'd never quite be accepted by them, try as I might—terrified the while of washing up with the ugly, the abandoned, the mad of the world . . . bearing in mind that my only brother, after all, was Scott.

I ONLY HAVE a few fleeting impressions of Scott from the mid-eighties, though we didn't entirely lose touch. I saw him over the holidays, or got the odd letter. Soon after our fight in the parking lot, he lost his job at the restaurant and couldn't find another for a long while. The word was out. In the meantime he sponged off our mother and pursued an interest in petty larceny. When hungry he'd sometimes skulk around the suburbs until he found a backyard barbecue in progress; timing, he told me, was everything. He liked his meat at least medium rare, so he'd have to wait three or four minutes after the steaks or chickens or burgers were flipped, before bolting out of nowhere and fleeing with his dinner impaled on a stick. More serious burglaries had an ulterior motive—that is, Scott liked being in other people's houses: he was curious to see how they lived, what sort of pictures they hung on their walls, what their family photos revealed (was there a daughter?). He'd sneak into a given house around 2:00 A.M., and if there weren't any immediate alarums, he'd often stay most of the night. He also liked stealing from hospitals—pharmaceuticals, of course, but also mundane supplies such as bandages and surgical tubing. Marlies still has a wholesaler's box of petroleum jelly that he gave her once for her birthday: "This stuff really works," he remarked, "and keeps forever." For a while he was able to curb his thievery after he won a $20,000 settlement from a punk rock club, where the bouncer had broken his jaw in what Scott's lawyer insisted was an act of unwarranted aggression. The money, however, was squandered on vices that left him somewhat worse for wear.

I CAN'T REMEMBER how I first learned of Scott's religious conversion, but he'd taken to attending raucous services at the Crossroads Church, a place roughly the size of an NBA basketball arena. Scott liked that sort of thing and saw the humor in it too. Jimmy Swaggart became a great personal hero of his, all the more so when it came to light that the great televangelist liked to beat off in the presence of prostitutes. Aptly, perhaps, the person who turned Scott on to Swaggart, and hence religion, was none other than good old Uncle Ronny, who used to take such a childlike delight in naughty jokes ("There's no *fuck* in strawberry"). By then many of my mother's gay crowd were casualties of the AIDS epidemic, and Ronny had accepted God into his heart as a tribute to his own deliverance. Both he and my brother were able to reconcile a heartfelt faith with a lifestyle that remained dubious at best. Swaggart had proven that one could be born again and still stray from the path of righteousness on occasion.

I was relieved to find that Scott seemed, at first, disinclined to proselytize. For a year or so, his only sign of piety was the little cross-and-heart emblem with which he signed letters, always, from that point on. Then one bright chilly day around Christmas we were walking downtown to meet our father for lunch when Scott came to a dramatic stop on the sidewalk and shook me a little too roughly by the shoulders. He was beaming. He said we needed to "save" our father.

"You think he needs saving?" I asked.

"Well *yeah*, Zwieb. Otherwise he's going to hell."

I wasn't offended. I could see Scott was absolutely in earnest, and besides I was finished being offended by him, at least on the subject of our father.

"I have to disagree," I said. "If there's a hell, I really doubt Papa is going there. You know? I just can't picture it."

"*If* there's a hell . . . ?"

"Right. If."

"Aren't you a Catholic, Zwieb?"

He said this in a puzzled way, with perhaps the vaguest hint of distaste—the distaste of an evangelical Protestant for the Whore of Babylon—but mostly puzzled, since he'd clearly assumed I'd be an ally in this respect. Alas, my brief dabbling in religion was a thing of the past, and I told him so. Scott looked a little hurt, a little worried for me.

"Why?"

The answer, I suppose, was that my "faith" had been a pretty empty business to begin with, little more than a half-baked juvenile idealism that had lapsed for good my junior year in college, assisted by a girlfriend who preferred to stay in bed and have sex on Sunday mornings.

"It just, I don't know, it passed. I mean, for one thing, the whole idea of *hell* is ridiculous to me. Why would our father, for example, a good man who's worked hard all his life to support a family"—this a bit pointedly—"go to hell?"

"Because he's not saved!" Scott said with cheerful conviction.

We debated the point a little further, then abruptly (running late) Scott changed the subject somewhat.

"I think he was pretty shocked to hear about it."

"Hear about what?"

"My being *saved*. I mean if *I* can be saved, *any*one can!"

"You may have a point there," I said.

My brother laughed. "Exactly! I think he's ready to receive Jesus, Zwieb. I think I really made him think about things."

Scott didn't mention Jesus during lunch at the Petroleum Club that day except obliquely, when he said a hasty good-bye as we got up to leave. He had to go home and watch Swaggart, he explained, with an anxious glance at his watch.

Later my father and I sat chatting in his office, and I mentioned Scott's plan to "save" him.

"How do you think you'll respond to that?" I asked.

My father doffed his glasses and sat rubbing the bridge of his nose. "Like a cobra's been thrown at my feet," he said, with a quick wincing grin.

"He thinks you're pretty 'shocked' about the whole thing."

"No." He put his glasses back on. "I just assume his life got so bad there was nothing else to cling to."

AND STILL MY brother's life remained bleak in spite of his faith, and once again our family began to dread the sight and sound of him. There was always some petty disaster, some fresh grotesquerie—as when he complained to Sandra of "black shit." By then she'd taken to screening my father's calls (including the ones from me, if I made the mistake of calling him at home), and once, in the midst of Scott's flustered insistence that she let him speak to his "own *father*, goddammit," he mentioned that his shit was turning black. Poor Sandra hung up in a panic.

Finally he stopped calling. Though Scott would always believe we owed him love and patience no matter what, he must have known he wasn't wanted, and his pleas for attention only made it worse. For a year or so, all but our mother stopped hearing from him—though she heard plenty: a torrent of grief and grievance that almost drowned her capacity to respond in kind. Whenever possible she'd enlist old friends to bear part of the burden, people who tried to minister to Scott as the darling boy they'd once known—hence a photo of Walid from that desert era: his back to the camera, he stands in my mother's kitchen and clutches Scott's hand. The latter looks stricken but receptive. What was Walid saying?

BY MY SENIOR year at Tulane I was spending less and less time at the fraternity house. I'd come to accept that I didn't much like the majority of my brethren, and vice versa, and I'd had enough of sitting around the steps sipping beer and talking shit and shouting flirtatious abuse at the passing "talent" en route to the Josephine Louise dormitory on the Newcomb campus across Broadway. Two things occupied the better part of my time: an honors thesis on Walker Percy that I worked at pretty diligently, especially that second semester when deadlines loomed, and a tortured involvement with a quirky, troubled, and quite lovely girlfriend named Kate, from West Virginia, who shared my social exile to some extent. The year before, as a freshman, she'd pledged Pi Beta Phi but failed to make grades, and didn't really belong there anyway, so now she was all the more dependent on me and the odd boy she'd dally with on the side. We had terrible fights, the like of which I've never repeated with anyone. I don't think I could if I tried. I used it all up—the passion or heat or what you will, the incredulous shock one feels on first learning that others are just as corrupt as oneself. Suffice it to say, Kate and I had some good times too: when she wasn't screaming at me (after exhaustive provocation) in her Appalachian Betty Boop voice—"*Acehoe!*" (asshole)—she'd watch TV and needlepoint an elaborate SAE fraternity crest, suitable for framing, in a droll attempt to be the kind of girlfriend she thought I wanted (even as I became less and less the person who wanted that sort of thing), or, on weekends, we'd buy magazines and comics and whiskey and spend the night tippling in the big claw-foot tub I had in my Garden District apartment.

So the year passed, and despite completing a thesis that my adviser called "a model of the form," and graduating with low-level honors, I was still a very confused and stunted young man. All the more confused and stunted, perhaps, with every passing day.

After college I moved to Washington, D.C., I know not why. That first month I lived in a townhouse next door to the Dixie Pig Barbecue in Alexandria; to be exact, I lived in a room a little bigger than a closet with a twin-sized mattress on the floor. My three housemates were recent graduates of OU—also fraternity boys, as I recall. A paralegal in my father's office had put me in touch with them, since I hardly knew a soul in Washington. One was named Scott, and the only reason that sticks in my head is because he shared a name with my brother, who otherwise might have been a different species—nay, from a different planet in a distant (and really much nicer) galaxy. On weekends, when Scott #2 and the others would get drunk in their colorless way, they'd clatter down to the basement, where I was watching TV for want of anything better to do, and indulge in a little bedtime ritual: swaying slightly on the carpet, baseball caps over their hearts, they'd stand watching (over and over) the 1984 Reagan campaign ad set to the tune of Lee Greenwood's "God Bless the USA." I didn't comment; I didn't mention that I was a Democrat who'd voted for Mondale, nor did I point out that I'd been raised in a liberal family and spent the best times of my childhood in the company of gay men. I just sat there and wondered, in effect: *what the fuck.* The question was directed at me rather than them.

Meanwhile I worked as an intern in the office of Don Nickles, the baby-faced junior senator from Oklahoma. A Republican of the most guileless, God-fearing variety, Nickles had appointed my father as the token Democrat on a federal judiciary review board; otherwise I would have been an even more improbable member of his workforce. For a few weeks, though—for the sake of my father and certain vague ambitions—I did my best to fit in. I even attended one of Don's weekly Bible meetings in his office; I can't remember what we discussed, only that Don (as he insisted we call him) responded very politely to whatever ass-kissing, disingenuous piety I'd advanced: "That's a very interesting point, Blake . . ." He was a nice guy. Aside from (elective) Bible meetings, my job entailed answering the phone, entering data from the *Congressional Record*, and writing thoughtful, well-researched letters to constituents such as the woman from Broken Arrow who'd complained about airport noise. My letter to her was such a triumph of obliging, knowledgeable niceness that Senator Nickles himself, rather than the appropriate legislative assistant, saw fit to sign it. That, for me, was the high point.

I pretty much decided to rest on that laurel. Quite aside from Don's politics, which struck me as odious, the whole ethos seemed ill-suited to the wisenheimer I was. When I was answering phones, for example, I shared the reception area with a young woman named Nikky—a Baptist, of course, who was mystified or downright appalled by any observation that failed to confirm her own sunny but rather stern view of the world. Once, when her boyfriend had been "mean" to her in some way that seemed benign to me, he showed up in the office wearing a rented knight-errant costume and bearing (a) flowers and (b) a boombox playing "Lady," by Kenny Rogers. He got down on one knee and begged Nikky's forgiveness while everyone in the office gathered around laughing and clapping—it was *so* cute—and really, you know, that's what it took with Nikky! My own hands clapped mechanically, but I thought *What the fuck what the fuck what the fuck* . . . this, again, directed at me rather than them.

I knew the jig was up when I entered the Hart Building elevator one morning—at least fifteen minutes late, as usual, and getting later every day—and found myself face-to-face with Don, who murmured, "Good morning, Blake," in a markedly sorrowful way, the nearest thing to a snub he could muster. Sure enough there was a note on my desk from Don's administrative assistant, Doyce, a lanky freckled fellow with a reddish white man's 'fro.

Doyce greeted me, all smiles, a vacuous-looking Kurt Vonnegut, and asked me to shut the door. He was poring over my résumé and shaking his head.

"Says here you graduated with honors from Tulane! Heck, that's a good school! Bet you could get just about any job you wanted with this."

I gave sort of a demurring whimper, and Doyce got down to brass tacks. His smile faded into a pained look, as though he were passing something sharp in his stool. He wondered, rhetorically, whether my heart was really in the job anymore: my daily tardiness hadn't gone unnoticed, and just in general my comportment seemed a little . . . but Doyce was too nice a guy to take any pleasure in reproaching me, and whatever he was about to say dwindled into a wince. But finally he came out with it.

"Apparently, Blake, you've been telling our constituents over the phone to vote for George Nigh?"

Nigh was then governor of Oklahoma, a Democrat, and Don's opponent in the next election. I certainly preferred Nigh's politics to Don's, but honestly I couldn't remember making the comment in question, so I protested my innocence with a sweaty little Nixon-giggle. It was dawning on me all at once that they really, really disliked me in that office, and it seemed absurd to defend myself.

"You were overheard by a . . . by a pretty reliable source, Blake."

Nikky. Well, that made sense. Probably I'd mentioned Governor Nigh in a way that didn't entirely savor of rebuke, a seemly loathing, and to Nikky's pea-brain that was tantamount to a ringing endorsement. Anyway, I was out; no use refuting a paragon like Nikky. Doyce and I agreed to disagree and manfully shook hands. I heard him wadding up my résumé as I walked down the hall.

By then I'd moved to the paneled, fluorescent-lit basement of a ranch house in Arlington, which I shared with a large, unhappy woman named Faye and her fifteen-year-old daughter. Once upon a time Faye had taught at my high school in Oklahoma; we were mutual friends with a gay theology teacher, Mr. Osborn, who used to serve me whiskey from a porcelain teakettle when we'd meet twice a month (independent study) to discuss medieval philosophy and the like. Faye, I gathered, had moved to the D.C. area for the benefit of a bureaucrat husband who'd recently abandoned her, though he still came around for dinner once or twice a week and seemed very depressed about things. As for the daughter, she was more pissed off than depressed, as I learned one day when she came home from school and caught me upstairs watching *her* TV.

Earlier that summer my girlfriend Kate had practically begged for the privilege of shacking up with me in Washington—she was flunking out of Newcomb, and wanted a year off to consider her options—but now it was *quite* the other way around: come live with me, Kate (I all but cried), and be my feckless love! Nothing doing. Kate had visited me that first week in Alexandria and seen my mattress on the closet floor, the Dixie Pig Barbecue, my three leering housemates, and when she visited Arlington a month later and saw that things were, if anything, even worse, she decided to stay put with her eccentric mum in West Virginia. I couldn't blame her, of course, in my heart of hearts, though I blamed her roundly in person and over the phone.

Those last weeks in Arlington were perhaps the loneliest I've ever known as an adult. I had no job, and no idea what sort of job I was capable of holding, if any. For my twenty-second birthday Burck had given me a spiffy new VW Jetta, which I drove up and down the Potomac, all day and (mostly) all night, stopping at bars or scenic places to brood and read. I avoided Faye's house in Arlington as much as possible; my constant aloneness embarrassed me, and I wanted them to think (but why?) that I had somewhere to go. Midafternoon I'd come home briefly to shower, perhaps filch a few pieces of meat from a nasty, congealing stew in the fridge, then dress for a night on the town and drive away to nowhere again. I drove thousands of miles in just those two or three weeks, often tipsy, often lost; to this day I don't know my way around Washington any better than Timbuktu, such was the total daze I was in while exploring its every goat track. Not surprisingly my favorite book from this time was *A Fan's Notes*. I was feeling a keen affinity for Frederick Exley: his alcoholism, his morbid interest in sports, his contempt for the workaday world—the whole narcissistic juvenile whirl. It was hardly a stretch to see myself lying on a davenport reading *Lolita* for months on end, or cooling my heels in a madhouse, or even selling aluminum siding for Mr. Blue. That November, at any rate, I moved to New York, where I had a few friends at least, and was promptly hired as a waiter at the Morgan Bar, a tony crepuscular dungeon on Madison Avenue that had no liquor license because its owner (Steve Rubell of Studio 54 fame) was a felon.

DURING SCOTT'S ESTRANGEMENTS from the family, we used to speak of him with the kind of candor one reserves for the dead, when we spoke of him at all. My father and I would ritualistically mention him toward the latter stages of a given conversation, and one night our Scott-talk took a curious turn. This was in New York, where Burck had come on business and taken me out for a rare fancy meal at the Quilted Giraffe. As ever he asked if I'd heard anything lately, and I told him what little I knew. Then, with a kind of pensive amusement, my father asked if I thought Scott was gay.

I was taken aback; I smiled. "Why do you ask?"

"Well, I hear things," he said.

"Like what?"

"Well, for one thing, did you know he was here in New York recently?"

I did not.

"Well, he was. With—do you remember Kenny Harlan?"

I did: he'd been the youngest of my mother's gay crowd, the wispy scion of a wealthy vulgarian family (oil) who paid a remittance to keep him away. Kenny never worked or read a book or bothered much; as far as I could tell, his main occupation was getting drunk and poor-mouthing people until they beat the shit out of him. I suppose he was suicidal but lazy about getting on with it. Nonetheless I was startled to learn he was still alive, ten years later, and taking vacations with my brother.

"Old Kenny," I said. "How is he?"

"The same. Drunk off his ass. They stayed at the Chelsea."

We were both striving to keep up the casual tone. I didn't bother to ask how my father knew all this. He heard things.

"So what d'you think Krafft-Ebing would make of it?" he said.

"Well—" I paused. "I hardly think it *matters*..."

"I'm not saying it does."

This was misleading. Burck, to be sure, was nothing if not

liberal-minded, but at bottom he was still born and raised in Vinita, Oklahoma. Just because he was tolerant of homosexuality in
the abstract didn't mean he wanted a gay son, even an estranged
gay son. Though he was always kind to my mother's friends, and
amused by them, he worried about the whole scene. "God"—he
remarked to me once with a sigh—"I hope you don't turn into a
cocksucker."

I tried to put him at ease. "Scott's always talked about how
much he's bothered by gay men—'fucking faggots,' that sort of
thing. You remember what he said about Oscar."

"Who?"

"His roommate at NYU."

Any mention of NYU, in the context of Scott, made my father
wince. "Not sure I do."

"You know, he said Oscar wanted to fuck him. He said *everybody* wanted to fuck him, male or female. He said it bothered
him."

"Ah yes."

"On the other hand, Scott's pretty lonely these days, so who
knows. He and Uncle Ronny go to church together." I shrugged.
"But do I think he's gay? Nah. He likes girls, the younger the
better."

Then I mentioned Scott's obsession with various pubescent
starlets, his avid reading of *Tiger Beat* and the like. This for start-
ers. Finally, once I'd finished, my father changed the subject.

MY FIRST APARTMENT in New York was an eight-by-twelve
studio on the seventeenth floor of the George Washington Hotel
at Twenty-third and Lex. As I recall, it cost me $535 a month in
1986, or roughly half my take-home pay as an editorial assistant

at Cambridge University Press, where I'd begun working in the Behavioral and Brain Sciences division shortly after being fired from the Morgan Bar for absenteeism and general ineptitude. I didn't mind my tiny apartment—at least not at first. Sandra and I were in the midst of one of our brief détentes, and during a visit she'd urged Burck to buy me some streamlined Scandinavian furniture that made the most of my scant living space. The better part of my leisure, then, was spent reading on a thirty-inch-wide unvarnished wooden bed (with storage drawers); at my feet was a bookcase with a small TV in the middle compartment that I could watch when I got tired of reading. I rarely turned it on. I figured I'd better keep reading. Because of my promising honors thesis I'd decided to be a writer, though at the time I was mostly writing letters. Meanwhile I was often interrupted by an old lady next door, who on certain nights blasted Petula Clark's "Downtown" over and over again via the blown, raspy speakers of an ancient hi-fi. When I knocked on her door (diffidently) to protest, she appeared in a soiled housecoat and stocking cap; her face looked like the chalky bottom of a desiccated lake. Her eyes glittered. She gave me a garbled spiel about a noisy man in her ceiling who was trying to kill her by somehow smiting her on the forehead from above (she pantomimed this: smiting her forehead with the heel of her hand, rolling her eyes up into her head, and stumbling backward); Petula Clark helped drown the man's malicious racket, and since I wanted her to turn down the volume, I was pegged as another of her tormenters. "*Killer!*" she'd hiss, sitting on the steps leading from the lobby to the mailroom, where (she knew) I had to pass each day after work. I complained to the building manager, who said that they'd already been in touch with the woman's son in Baltimore. He wasn't eager to resume custody.

My boss at work was a gentle scholar named Susan, who appreciated my better qualities (such as they were) and quietly ignored my cadaverous hangovers. I'd never been to New York prior to my arrival that autumn, and mostly I was enchanted. Every block, even the squalid ones, struck me as a fresh romance. I remember discovering Gramercy Park and simply marveling: two blocks away I lived in a grungy residential hotel next door to a lunatic, and here was this fanciful square of grass and trees and quaint wrought-iron benches and somberly prosperous brownstones. I tried the gate: locked! *Mais bien sûr*, it was *right* to be locked; it was something to aspire to. I was still young! That seated madonna there on a bench, with her pram, she'd earned a key and I hadn't. I wished her well.

But a key would be long in coming, and soon I grew bitter. In college I'd been promising: I belonged to a good fraternity; I had a fetching, whimsical girlfriend; and finally I'd transcended my lifelong inertia and written an honors thesis that was deemed "a model of the form." And now? I was a bookish sluggard working for peanuts and learning the hard way that a decent undergraduate thesis was hardly a sound predictor of literary success. All the while I sensed that some terrible fall was imminent, and what sanctuary would I seek when it came? I was welcome at home (that is, barely tolerated) only for brief visits during the winter holidays; summer visits were arranged, tensely, on an ad-hoc basis. All this was tacitly understood.

I decided to spend the summer of 1987 with friends in Hermosa Beach, California. I'd just been accepted into the NYU graduate film school for the fall and was giddy with relief that my life was about to have some forward motion again; also I wouldn't have to write any more apprentice fiction, thank *God*. In the meantime I'd moved from the George Washington Hotel to a nice apartment near the UN with my best friend, Mike (my best friend *to this day*, I hasten to add, with pride and amazement). Mike was dating a dancer/actress who'd done rather well on Broadway and knew a lot of other show-business people. It was a Saturday in late May, and I was in my cubicle at Cambridge University Press for the last time, tying up loose ends for Susan, my boss, who'd been so kind to me. Mike phoned me at work: his dancer girlfriend was having a big party at her raffish penthouse in Spanish Harlem, and so-and-so (a famous actor who went on to become more famous still) was expected to put in an appearance; what say I tip the remaining contents of my in-box into the trash and join them? This I did, more or less, and proceeded to get massively hammered. There was a lot to celebrate, after all, not least my relief at being able to say—to actors, no less—"I'm going to NYU Film School" instead of "I'm in the Behavioral and Brain Sciences division at Cambridge University Press." The famous guy never showed up, but I did get into a lively chat with an older soap-opera actor (bald, handlebar mustache) who claimed to be a mentor to this celebrity, who was an ingrate, he said, and a bitch.

Next thing I knew I was sharing a cab with this fellow, since we were both heading downtown, and he asked whether I wanted to grab a quick drink in the Village. It was maybe six in the evening; I said sure. Then I was in a leather bar on Christopher Street near the Hudson River, chatting with an enormous fellow in a motorcycle cap who stared impassively at the back of the bar while I wondered aloud whether it was wise for him and gay men generally to cultivate such a lifestyle in this day and age. I might even have mentioned my mother's old friends—my darling uncles, so many departed, etc. Probably I wept a little. The sun was a faint disappearing orange over the river.

Then it was dark and eight hours later, and I was riding in a cab with a pregnant prostitute. I have never recovered those eight hours in any form; the soap-opera actor, later canvassed by Mike, said he'd left after a single drink, while I'd insisted on staying and maybe talking sense into that guy with the motorcycle cap. If the latter got revenge for my egregious little homily by fixing me up with a pregnant, malodorous (some kind of hair stuff and a hard night's sweat), and quite pimply prostitute, well then I gratefully salute him across the years: it might have been *so* much worse, and God knows some kind of reprisal was in order. Or maybe I slept at the leather bar for six or seven hours and then endeavored to pick up this person under my own steam; friends tell me I can be eerily articulate in the midst of my blackouts. But I'll never know. Simply I came to in a cab and there she was. Then we were back at my apartment and she was naked, and very pregnant, and I gave her some money and begged off, whereupon she slept in my bed. I slept in the other room. Mike, thank God, had spent the night at his dancer's apartment.

Picture our little tableau in the morning. The prostitute made herself at home, taking a long shower and teasing her 'fro as best she could with Mike's brush. I sat reading the *Times* at a little table next to the partial wall between kitchen and living room, while she came and went—naked, flat-footed, dripping—helping herself to the contents of our fridge. I was loath to get on her bad side. She knew where I lived; doubtless she had a pimp. I read and wished her gone. Then I heard a key in the lock. "*Get back to the room!*" I hissed. "*Go! Now!*" My urgency must have alarmed her—maybe she thought a wife or a cop was at the door—and she trotted *flap flap flap* back to my bedroom, her jouncing naked body observed en passant by Mike from our partly opened, chain-locked door. I let him in. I whispered "Sorry about this," while he stood there with his mouth open, hands on either side of his head à la Edvard

Munch's *The Scream*. Presently the young woman emerged in her finery and quietly departed, belly first. The next day I left New York for the summer.

I SAW MY brother again a year later—when all was changed, changed utterly. In the preceding months Marlies had mentioned that Scott was now in California—Mississippi—Hawaii (!)—because he'd joined the Marine Corps and seemed to be doing fine; this, I figured, was some bullshit story he'd fed the poor, gullible woman while leading a hobo life. Even if he'd managed to enlist, I gave him a couple of weeks, tops, before he was returned to the civilian world in a sprawling heap. Meanwhile I'd finished my one and only year at the NYU graduate film school; it cost me roughly $30,000 (I paid off the last of my loans in 2001) to learn I had little talent or interest in that direction and was, let's face it, lost. So that was that. For the time being, then, I was an incompetent, soon-to-be-fired bartender at an Italian restaurant in Norman, Oklahoma, seeing a lot more of my mother than either of us would have liked. As for Scott, well, picture my pop-eyed astonishment: for he was now, indeed, an ultracompetent aviation supply clerk on leave from his Marine Corps base in Kaneohe, Hawaii. He looked good, too: his face had a glow, and most of his pimples were gone, with little apparent scarring unless you saw him under a certain light. Looking good, in fact, was the one thing we had in common—I was getting a lot of sun—and my favorite photo of us, sitting side by side on my mother's couch, was taken around that time: Scott seems tickled but magnanimous too, clasping my knee in a consoling sort of way; I don't seem particularly depressed, perhaps because of my tan.

Ten or so months before, Scott's pariahdom was complete: all but my mother had disowned him, he couldn't find a job, and even his more sordid friends kept away. When the last decent bar in town had eighty-sixed him for good, it was time to make a drastic change or give up entirely: the marines. Such was Scott's notoriety, though, that he thought better of attempting to enlist anywhere in his home state. Rather he drove (in *what* I have no idea) all the way to San Diego, drinking Jim Beam the while, or so he later told it.

I can only imagine what basic training must have entailed; I suppose he persevered out of sheer desperation, a total lack of options, to say nothing of the antic delight he must have afforded some drill sergeant. Anyway, he persevered. My mother went alone to his graduation, and such was my brother's lockstep conformity on the parade ground, his look of absolute belonging from behatted head to shining foot, that my mother spent the entire ceremony taking zoom photos of someone other than Scott, who finally tapped her on the shoulder as she made to embrace his doppelgänger. Afterward they took a trip to a friend's place near Joshua Tree in the desert, where my brother reverted to his old ways somewhat: for a solid week he did nothing but lie by the pool and drink, morosely, his Walkman buzzing loud enough to scare birds away—or so my mother said at the time.

After that, he went from strength to strength. In Meridian, Mississippi, he took a course in aviation supply and finished first in his class. He also proved a superior marksman: for months he competed all over the country with the marine pistol team, racking up medals, and soon became an instructor. Finally he got a plum assignment in Kaneohe, where he was dubbed the Sultan of Supply. It was simply miraculous—though like most miracles one could divine certain scientific explanations amid the mystery.

Scott, after all, was hardly the first misfit who'd found a degree of success in the military: as a supply clerk he was expected to sit in his cage and push paper, though he also seemed to possess a talent for doing efficient little favors at the right time, for the right person, regardless of protocol. In short he was popular and rather powerful after a fashion, and with his ego burnished for the first time in years, he didn't need to drink and drug so much. Nor did he have the time or energy. I imagine he spent the odd spot of leisure in his old manner, as in Joshua Tree with my mother—listening to music, skimming magazines or the Bible, tippling the while—but when he got back to work he behaved himself more or less. He had no choice.

YET AGAIN SCOTT was welcomed back into the bosom of the family. My father told me about their first meeting in over a year. Scott was so rattled he could scarcely finish a sentence; he coughed and made cryptic jokes, compulsively gulping his beer. Finally my father put a hand on his shoulder.

"What's wrong, son?"

"I guess I'm kinda *nervous*, Papa. I don't . . ."

Burck waited for him to finish, but Scott just shook his head and stared at his glass.

"You don't have to be nervous," my father said. "There's nothing to be nervous about. Everybody's happy to see you. We're proud of you."

My brother's eyes began to leak a little, but he was a marine now and kept his composure.

Another emotional moment was when I told him about enlarging that favorite photo of us (sitting, tanned, on Mom's couch) and pinning it over my bed. I'd mentioned it only in passing, in the course of a rare long-distance chat, after he'd asked me to describe my new digs in West Palm Beach—where I'd moved in the hope of starting over, or at least failing in relative obscurity (I was trying, again, to write). My apartment, the bottom floor of a carriage house, was furnished in a quirkily hideous way, and after I'd mentioned the lampstand shaped like a pile of limes, the cubist painting that my landlord had confessed to be his own work, the yellow sofa with its solemn brown stain, I added, "Oh! And there's a photo of us over the bed."

Pause. "What photo?"

"You know, the one Mom took last summer. The one of us on the couch. I made it into a poster and tacked it up. You're the first thing I see when I wake up in the morning, for better or worse."

Naturally I wanted my brother to be pleased that I'd put a photo of us (poster-sized, no less) over my bed, but also I expected him to see the humor of that feature in the midst of such a piquant, overall tackiness. And really the dismal fact of the matter was simply this: I'd hung that photo because I thought it flattered *me*, because I was badly in need of flattery at the time.

After a silence, my brother said "Wow" and let his breath out in a long hiss. "I really don't know what to say, Zwieb."

He was on the verge of tears over something that meant almost nothing to me. I did my best to change the subject.

I BEGAN TO fancy myself a kind of knockabout intellectual à la Frank Wheeler in *Revolutionary Road,* and thus I contrived to feel superior to certain old friends who'd surrendered themselves to the rat race. At bottom I was a failure and knew it better than anybody. When my worried father would call and ask how I was doing, I'd tell funny stories at my own expense to show him that my sense of humor, at least, was intact. Meanwhile he helped in whatever way he could—there was usually a check or a fifty-dollar bill enclosed with his letters—though it hurt and probably embarrassed him that his second-born son, something of a white hope up to then, was also having a bad time adjusting to the real world.

Things began to look up a little in West Palm Beach. Good old Mike was there, for one thing—my roommate and best friend in New York, that candidate for sainthood. He too was trying to write, and when I'd first mentioned the possibility of rejoining him in Florida, he replied with a nervous letter, the gist of which was: by all means come ahead; I'll even find you an apartment in advance (as he did); but I have a good life here, Blake, and I won't stand for your fucking it up. Fair enough! Probably it was best I hadn't told him too much about my last days in Norman. In a nutshell: having been fired at the Italian place and being left, once again, with way too much time on my hands, I'd begun making the long drive to Oklahoma City more and more often, the better to hang out with old high school friends—the unsuccessful ones, the ones who hadn't escaped—and naturally we drank quite a lot, whereupon I'd endeavor to drive all the way back to Norman in the wee, wee hours. This, of course, was downright suicidal, and bore the expected fruit. One night I slammed over a curb on the entrance ramp to I-35 and had to wait until sunrise near the Fifty-first Street exit with a mangled tire, woken every now and then by the shuddering blast of a passing eighteen-wheeler; I was too drunk to work the jack (tricky little gadgets in those old VWs), and finally was rescued by my mother's boyfriend, Dave, who stopped on his way to work the next morning. Then one night—maybe a week later?—I came back to my blah apartment with the dirty carpet and cinder-block bookshelves and decided I was hungry, so I put a pot of water on the stove to boil spaghetti and passed out. I woke up, hours later, to a mortal stench: the bottom of the pot had melted on the burner, and little metallic embers were flying all over the place; the smoldering carpet was ruined, and surely would have burst into flames if I'd slept a bit longer. I had a slight cough for weeks after. Finally, a few days before my departure for Florida, I fell asleep at the wheel of my Jetta and plowed into the back of another, bigger car. This on I-35 again, late at night. The collision woke me, and sobered me, and when the police arrived I was quite alertly contrite and they let me off with a ticket.

If I'd stayed in Oklahoma a few more weeks, I daresay I might have managed to kill myself. At any rate I wouldn't be writing this; I'm pretty sure of that.

Through all of this, my brother was a comfort to me. He was perhaps the one person on earth who genuinely admired me— was even somewhat in awe: he thought I was "brilliant" because I'd graduated from a decent college with honors, or perhaps because I'd done so in spite of being laden with many of the same flaws that had made his own life such a dreary business. In letters he went out of his way to suggest I'd be a success in the long run, while the best he could hope for was a kind of "functioning mediocrity"—this, I might add, amid the usual epistolary quirkiness: his analysis of, say, a *Rolling Stone* article about some washed-up rocker (enclosed with a lot of scribbled marginalia); bits of scripture that had particularly puzzled or pleased him; some actress (invariably pubescent) whom he loved and wanted me to love too.

I repaid my brother's kindness as best I could, responding to his letters at droll, deadpan length: "I, too, laughed at Robin Gibb's remark that 'How Deep Is Your Love' refers to a cavernous vagina (though I wonder whether such ribaldry is the best way to jump-start a career)" . . . "as for what Christ said about the camel and the needle's eye, well, I doubt people are damned just because they die wealthy, and besides that's nothing you or I need to worry about" . . . "per your advice, I watched that new show the other night with particular attention to [some pubescent actress], though really I found her a little too androgynous for my taste, at least at this stage in her . . ." It wasn't simply a question of humoring Scott, since he was in on the joke—that is, he *knew* his interests were eccentric and sensed I was being ironical; at the same time, these *were* his actual interests, and he enjoyed discussing them at sober length, irony or no.

Mainly I was amusing myself. I was out of touch with most of my old friends and simply had few people to write, apart from family and the wayward Kate, who rarely wrote back. When I wasn't chatting with Mike and his fiancée, Donna, I was waiting tables (prior to being fired) or writing (badly) or reading or walking along Lake Worth and/or drinking. The last usually involved lying in the dark and listening to music I associated with better days, though I continued to believe that some sort of heady redemption lay ahead. In the last half hour or so before passing out, my reveries would take a maudlin turn: for instance, I liked to imagine thanking my parents in some grandiose public way for having never given up on me during my errant salad days. Also I spent my drinking time making mix tapes, mostly for my brother, who wrote astute critiques on the quality of my playlists as well as their rationale, the way they seemed to reflect my present state of mind. Sometimes I'd make the matter explicit by singing a few songs into the boombox microphone, the more lugubrious the better (e.g., Barry Manilow's "Trying to Get the Feeling Again")—a joke that wasn't entirely a joke, as I knew Scott would appreciate.

MY BROTHER ENDED up in Okinawa, where he took a course in broadcast journalism and made some extra money teaching English to Japanese businessmen. (He was flush enough to send me two hundred dollars—badly needed—for my twenty-eighth birthday in 1991.) He got his own show on an armed forces radio station and also had some kind of gig as an emcee at military award banquets. Around that time, too, he received NCO Leadership and Good Conduct medals, as well as a framed souvenir record album on the occasion of his discharge in 1992, signed with obvious affection by his radio colleagues.

Scott sent me a tape of his radio show, presumably a broadcast he was proud of. I listened to it once, while cooking dinner, then put it away until recently. Scott's radio manner struck me as wooden, though it's possible he was expected, as a marine, to dispense with the usual deejay patter. It also occurs to me that Scott was mindful of his privilege—his own show!—to an almost morbid degree, such that he was cautious not to make any risky remark, to give any hint of an unbalanced nature. There's a comic incongruity between the Scott-ishness of the musical program (AC/DC's "Highway to Hell" followed by a Dusty Springfield tune) and Scott's monotone delivery throughout: "I have a request from Staff Sergeant Mike Berry for two tickets to the New Year's Eve dance tomorrow night at the armory. That's two tickets to the New Year's Eve dance. If anybody can help Sergeant Berry, please call me here at the station. That's two tickets . . ." Only once does Scott allow a touch of his personality to intrude—toward the end of the show, when he plays Roy Clark's 1969 recording of "Yesterday When I Was Young": "It's a little corny," Scott remarks with a self-conscious chuckle, "but I like it a lot. It's got a kind of poignance for this time of year."

. . . The thousand dreams I dreamed, the splendid things I
  planned
I always built to last on weak and shifting sand.
I lived by night and shunned the naked light of the day
and only now I see how the years ran away . . .
Yesterday the moon was blue
and every crazy day brought something new to do.
I used my magic age as if it were a wand
and never saw the waste and emptiness beyond . . .
The friends I made all seemed somehow to drift away
and only I am left on stage to end the play.
There are so many songs in me that won't be sung,
I feel the bitter taste of tears upon my tongue.
The time has come for me to pay for yesterday when I was young.

SHORTLY BEFORE HIS thirty-second birthday, Scott was honorably discharged with the rank of lance corporal. We wondered about his decision not to reenlist at a time when he seemed to be doing so well, but Scott explained he had little hope of promotion because of recent cuts in the defense budget. Besides, he had a number of irons in the fire: he was making "decent scratch" as a language teacher (he showed me his business card, which certainly looked professional: Japanese on one side, English on the other), and meanwhile he and a friend had started a production company, which didn't pan out for one reason or another.

Years later, in a bizarre coincidence, my aunt Kay struck up a conversation on a plane with an ex-marine who, it turned out, had been stationed in Okinawa with my brother; in fact they'd been pretty good friends.

"Scott was a nice guy," the man said, "but he had a lot of problems." Something in my aunt's manner had suggested, perhaps, that such an observation wasn't wholly unexpected, but still the man felt obliged to explain: "He drank a lot. A *lot*. We tried to get him some help, but Scott—" He shook his head.

Another revealing item was an alumni bulletin I received from our old high school while Scott was still a marine. I noticed he was listed among the Notes for the Class of '83—five years later than he'd actually graduated. When I mentioned this to my father, he penetrated the matter with his usual lucidity.

"I imagine Scott misreported his age."

"But why?"

"Well," my father sighed, a little exasperated at having to say as much, "I guess he's embarrassed about being a thirty-year-old corporal."

And this was two years before Scott decided not to reenlist— still a corporal. My father thinks he was basically drummed out of the service, though nothing of the sort appears in his record (perhaps that was part of the deal) and my mother waxes indignant at any such insinuation: "Oh *bullshit*," she says. "You guys just don't want to give Scott credit for *anything*. He was a *wonderful* marine . . ."

The truth of Scott's military career is somewhere in between, I think: yes, he was a good marine, and yes, it ended badly. He didn't want to be a thirtyish corporal; he didn't want to be thirtyish period. Scott's acceptance of his own mediocrity was deceptive. During his vagrant days he lived in a realm of pure possibility: he could be anything he wanted, if only he tried. Then he tried and became a thirtyish marine corporal in Okinawa, albeit one who did cool things like deejay his own show and emcee award banquets. When Scott discovered this wasn't enough, and wasn't likely to get better, that may have been the biggest disaster of all.

———

HE INSISTED ON returning to Oklahoma for the very reason that, arguably, he should have stayed away: he knew a lot of people there. My mother tried to remonstrate with him ("Don't be ridiculous! Stay in Japan!"), but Scott held his ground and even moved in with her for a few months until he got settled. As for my father, he welcomed Scott home by giving him the old BMW, that car he and Sandra had shipped back from Europe the same summer Scott had dabbled in smack and landed in rehab.

Beneath our hopefulness was a coral reef of accumulated cynicism, though of course we didn't concede as much even to ourselves; we simply knew what we knew. I mention this to suggest the shock we felt when Scott really did show signs of making good. Within a month he'd landed a paid internship in the news department of a local TV station. The pay wasn't much ($7.50 an hour), but he was eligible for a salaried position if he worked out, and meanwhile he was allowed to do those five-second spots between commercials: "Pit bulls on the loose! Two roving pit bulls have been killing cats in Nichols Hills. News at ten." This in the polished nasal monotone he'd perfected as a marine deejay. Before long, almost everyone we knew in Oklahoma City had seen Scott on TV and assumed he was on his way to becoming a celebrity of sorts. What a turnaround!

I was living in New Orleans, trying to get my teaching certificate. Over the years my stock had continued to drop vis-à-vis my stepfamily, despite efforts to support myself and become, belatedly, the kind of unassuming guy who knows he doesn't amount to much and makes no bones about it. At this rate, though, Scott would eclipse me both as a family member *and* worldly success. It was a little surreal.

Then one night I got a strange message on my machine. At the time I always screened my calls, since there were few people I wanted to talk to, and I was usually a little drunk at night. This particular caller, a young woman with a nebulous foreign accent, seemed to know I was listening as she spoke.

"This is Miriam," she said. (Actually, as I later learned, she spelled it *Maryam*.) She sounded as though she'd been crying and was now tensely composed. She paused, perhaps in the hope I'd pick up. "I am in New Orleans." Pause. "Please tell Scott to call me." Pause. "Or I will kill myself."

I bolted to my feet and fumbled with the phone, but she'd hung up after that fourth and final pronouncement.

"What's going on?" my mother said, when I called and asked to speak to Scott.

"Nothing. I just want to talk to my brother, for God's sake. Put him on, please."

"*What's going on?*"

But finally she passed the phone to Scott.

"Zwieb?" His voice was furtive; I heard a door click shut. "What's up?"

I could tell he already knew the gist of it. "Who *is* that woman?" I asked. "She crazy? Why's she calling *me*?"

My brother implied with a chuckle that, yes, she *was* a little crazy and this wasn't the first time she'd threatened to kill herself. Therefore we could all relax. He told me she was on vacation in New Orleans with her fuckwad husband, and Scott thought she might enjoy meeting me. This by way of explaining how she got my number in the first place and why she thought to call me in the midst of her latest despair—that is, Scott had refused to give her our mother's number, though he was worried about her and eager to return her call so he could explain to her, once again, why life was worth living. Before hanging up he made me promise not to tell our parents, and I made him promise not to give my number to any more of his crazy girlfriends.

THAT SUMMER I went home and saw my brother for the first time since his discharge. Except for his drinking he seemed fine— a statement that also applied to myself, for better and for worse: I was working hard at my education classes, desperate for steady employment, and meanwhile I went through a fifth of liquor every two or three days. As for Scott, the only cloud on his horizon that I could see was our mother's determination to keep him from the same blithe hobby. God knows she was a formidable obstacle by then: she'd become portly around the age of fifty and was now a vigorous 190 pounds of farmhand fat and muscle. A few years ago she'd moved from her condo to a place in the country where she could keep animals and do her gardening and whatnot; my brother named this haven "Womanhood" (because he called our mother Woman in the same whimsical spirit that he called me Zwieb) and was forever threatened with eviction if he couldn't stay reasonably sober.

I was taken aback by the sight of my brother's car—that is, Burck's old BMW: dusty and disheveled, its lovely burgundy finish was now marred by a savage key-scrape around its entire circumference (the work of Maryam's fuckwad husband). During its ten years in my father's care, the car had looked as sleek as the day it rolled off the boat, but once Scott assumed ownership it became like a schizophrenic taken off meds. One by one its nifty little features went on the fritz: the thermostat, the cruise control, the miscellaneous gizmos. Scott loved the car and assured me he'd have it repainted as soon as he could "muster the dosh";

meanwhile he kept the stereo in working order and the car raced around town like a bellowing hobo.

One day I visited Scott at that TV station where he still worked as an intern. He'd asked me to bring him something, but the real point was to watch him being taped for one of those five-second news spots. He didn't sit on the set where the regular anchor sat; rather he was propped on a stool with the busy newsroom visible behind him. For my benefit he bantered with a couple of harried PA's who fixed his clip-on microphone and adjusted the teleprompter: "C'mon, let's *do* this thing . . . Tom, can I get some coffee here? . . . Do I look pretty? Man! You ever *seen* anybody this pretty? . . ."

And so on, as if he were terribly bored with the whole business but willing to be good-humored about it. A lovable old pro. In fact it *was* rather impressive the way his manner changed as soon as taping began: his face went blank and he nailed it on the first take; then, the moment it was over, he plucked off his mic and sauntered away like Sinatra. The others responded to Scott with a kind of meek, long-suffering patience—he was older than they, and vaguely dangerous, and besides they seemed to know (even if Scott didn't) that they wouldn't have to suffer him much longer.

Sure enough he was fired the following week. Having seen what I saw, I wasn't surprised; as for Scott, he affected to be at peace with it. "*Such* a bullshit job," he said, going on about what an "embarrassment" it was to be associated with such a "poorly managed" enterprise. I replied that the competence of management wasn't his immediate concern as an intern, a point he seemed to concede with a little chuckle. He asked me not to tell our mother about it, and for weeks he continued to leave her house "to go to work," until finally he moved into a rental home owned by our father.

———

BURCK WAS PAINFULLY aware that Sandra and her children didn't like me and only tolerated Scott, but he wouldn't let go of the hope that sooner or later we'd come to appreciate each other's finer qualities. To that end he organized a family trip to Santa Fe for Christmas in 1992—the first time in years we were all together for more than a day or so, and this time Scott was included.

Two nights before I boarded the plane to New Mexico, I got in a bar fight. After a long season of cloistered tippling I was restless, and ended up sucker-punching a guy who'd called me a faggot during a pool game. Turned out he had a lot of friends. Happily the damage was mostly internal, a few creaky ribs, though I had enough of a shiner at the airport to confirm Sandra's view of me as a dissolute character. My father held me off after a welcoming hug and whistled. I said he should see the other guy, that I'd been defending a friend and so forth (though of course the opposite was true, and in fact the episode had strained the one good friendship I had in New Orleans). While I stood there, quipping and lying, I happened to glance at Sandra's face: for a moment it seemed pinched with such loathing—before flashing back to a tired smile—that I wondered if I'd hallucinated it. Her children were already heading off to Baggage Claim.

It was no hallucination. That night at dinner I found that if I looked away from Sandra even for a moment, her face would resume its scowl, a spectral presence in my peripheral vision. As for Kelli and Aaron, I couldn't bear to look at them at all. For a while I spoke to my father as though he were the only one at the table, until his face hardened in such a way as to suggest I include the others. I managed a smile and turned to Kelli.

"So Kelli. What're you up to these days?"

"What're *you* up to these days?"

That was worse than I'd expected, and whatever I managed to stammer about my teaching certificate, etc., came out as disingenuous, affected, self-congratulatory—whatever bad thing they wanted it to be. When I was done Kelli went on talking to her brother as though she'd been pointlessly interrupted.

Scott arrived the next day, and we all went skiing. My father and I were decent intermediates, Kelli and Sandra could wend their way down the green slopes in a wary snowplow, Aaron was a hot-dog, and Scott had never skied in his life. Still he insisted on taking the main lift to the top of the mountain without so much as a single lesson. Our father patiently explained to him about bending his knees and traversing to break his speed, whereupon Scott wobbled a few yards and fell down. Thus he descended in bruising increments. For my part I was glad to find I'd lost none of my old skill: I'd ski within inches of where Scott lay sprawled after his latest wipeout and swish a bit of powder onto his prone form; once, while he was struggling to get up, I jumped over him as if I couldn't wait for him to get out of the way. Scott seemed to take it all in stride.

Finally, after we'd left him on the bunny slope with a beginners' class, my father turned to me on the lift. His face was flushed with more than the cold.

"Stop making fun of him!"

I was startled by his vehemence, and muttered something about how Scott of all people could take a joke.

My father shook his head. "It's not *good* for him. He doesn't *need* that right now. Don't you think his self-esteem is banged up enough as it is?"

I could scarcely doubt my father's sincerity, but I still thought he was overreacting. I said it wasn't a question of "self-esteem":

Scott had never gone skiing, for heaven's sake; there was no reason he should expect to be any good. My father just shook his head and lapsed into a glowering silence. Years would pass before I finally got it: Scott's incompetence as a skier, to which I had the bad taste to advert, was due to the fact that he'd never been welcome in the old days, when my father and I had taken a number of ski trips while Scott was banished, down and out. Our relative skill was a reminder that for long periods of time we'd conducted our lives entirely separate from his, as if he didn't exist.

THAT NIGHT, AFTER our parents went to bed, Scott and I abolished whatever benefit of the doubt our stepsiblings were willing to grant us. In the hotel bar for a nightcap, we made it clear to Kelli and Aaron that we meant to drink until we got drunk, and moreover to charge these drinks to our rooms (and hence our father). *Room*, rather: whereas Kelli and Aaron had separate rooms, Scott and I had to share a single. For this reason and certain ineffable others, we felt entitled, and anyway we were too broke to pay the tab ourselves.

But then, our father's largesse was well-known to us all, the fact that he himself would hardly have minded: it was a vacation; it was Christmas; it was his treat. What Kelli and Aaron really wanted was a definite moral advantage, some rational vindication of a largely instinctive loathing.

"You're ordering *another*?" said Kelli.

Scott and I tapped glasses and nodded. The fullness of her reproach was suggested by her refusal to look at us, a lofty sidelong sigh. Aaron sipped his one stale beer. And still they remained to keep us company, perhaps to keep an eye on us, to commit our enormities to memory.

THE NEXT MORNING it was obvious they'd lost no time tat-
tling on us. The three of them, Sandra and her children, dourly
kept their distance; Kelli and Aaron seemed to be nursing their
mother through a wasting illness. I tried to comfort myself with
the thought that they despised me in good times and bad, drunk
or sober, whether I was inclined to ingratiate myself or not.
Hating me was dogma. As for Scott, he was simply weird and
not much of a threat, though his weirdness had long ago lost its
charm.

I wasn't sure how much my father knew about the night
before. It was possible Sandra had spared him the whole painful
tale of our lavish drinking, or perhaps he was simply making the
best of what was proving a pretty grim business. In any case he
seemed cheerful enough, if a bit worried by his wife's worsening
mood.

Sandra and her kids stayed in town that day to shop and commiserate; my father drove Scott and me to the ski basin without
them. I sat in the back of the car and brooded over the awfulness
of it all while we listened to a mix tape of country-western tunes
that Scott had made for our father. Scott was especially proud of
the segues between songs—part of his deejay training—the way
each song blended seamlessly into the next, how the whole tape
seemed a kind of continuous country-western symphony. "Listen to that!" he'd say, one trembling finger aloft. "*Shit*. Wasn't
that *perfect*?" I thought of my brother, unemployed these many
months, spending untold hours perfecting his segues; if Kelli and
Aaron were with us, no doubt they'd have rolled their eyes or,
worse, praised Scott exuberantly for his prowess. This increased
my sense of grievance, though of course I too found Scott's segue
talk ridiculous.

I wasn't much of a conversationalist as Burck and I rode the lift. In better days our incidental banter had been as easy as breathing, but now I felt sure my stepfamily was bent on dismantling our rapport piece by piece, until they could cart my father away, sift what they needed, and remake him in their own image. I was damned if I'd take it lying down.

"Look," I said, after we'd dismounted at the top of the mountain. "I'm tired of being the bad guy in this outfit. Those stepchildren of yours slander me every chance they get, and I've never said a word against them . . ."

This was partly true: while I sometimes tried to entice my father into admitting their less endearing qualities—he'd oblige me only in the vaguest way ("Kelli can be pretty strong mustard"; "school isn't Aaron's strong suit")—I was careful not to disparage them outright. But there on the slopes I opened the floodgates at last.

"I take a drink and the first thing they do is run to Mommy and tell her what a lush I am. I make a joke that Sandra doesn't like and the first thing she does is complain to her kids. And they talk about what a *drunk* I am, what a *shit* I am, what a *shame* it is that such a good man should have fathered two rotten sons. I'm sick of it! What'd I ever do to them?"

My father listened with weary patience, but what could he do that he hadn't done before? What could he say? Now and then he fogged the air with his unhappy sighs.

THAT NIGHT WAS Christmas Eve, and Sandra had wanted us to walk along the "Christmas Trail" that went past shops and quaint adobe cottages on Canyon Road, lined on either side with the little paper lanterns called farolitos. It was what one did on Christmas Eve in Santa Fe; she'd been looking forward to it. By the time we set out, though, she was markedly subdued, and I knew my father had tried talking to her about my various complaints. No doubt she'd rebutted him with a bitter account of my drinking the night before, which had led to God knows what. I was glad I hadn't been a fly on that wall.

The Christmas Trail was a sort of darkling carnival midway, with lots of Indians pretending to be picturesque local artisans, hawking their mass-produced wares. From either side of the flickering trail they leered and beckoned; jaded carolers were stationed at intervals along the path. Sandra's shoulders sagged beneath the serape she'd bought that afternoon for the occasion. I was careful not to say a word, though my brother felt no such compunction.

"I think I'll treasure this memory until the day I die, Zwieb . . . You carve that yourself?"—this to a cross-legged Indian who nodded guardedly, as though his English were none too good. "That guy back there carved one exactly like it! Is he your cousin or something? . . . Wow, this trail just goes on and on. Hell no, I don't want to turn around; I hope it goes on forever! Don't you, Zwieb?"

And he wasn't even drunk. The worst part was the way he included me in his mockery, as though we were in cahoots about finding this Christmas Trail (and by implication Sandra herself) the epitome of kitsch. Sandra walked along like Christ en route to Golgotha, supported on either side by her Samaritan children. For the moment she didn't want my father's comfort; he was to blame for bringing me into the world, after all.

"Well, it *seemed* like a nice idea," she'd sigh from time to time. "I just wanted everyone to have fun . . ."

All this was directed at me. As far as Sandra was concerned, my brother was little more than a hooting Id, a malicious puppet I used to torment her. And she may have had a point there, since his mockery was entirely for my benefit, and indeed the reason—or one reason—he hated her was because she hated me. Scott was nothing if not loyal.

And still there were four days left to our family vacation. We hastily opened presents after the Christmas Trail debacle, then went our separate ways. That meant I was stuck with Scott's company for the rest of the trip. My father had wisely decided to devote himself to mollifying his wife.

If you were with the adult Scott for only an hour or so, it's possible you'd leave the meeting with an impression of—well, not normalcy exactly, but a kind of refreshing eccentricity. Our first lunch alone together, the day after Christmas, was like that. We ate in the hotel restaurant (so we could charge the meal to our father) and drank nothing stronger than wine, which was enough to push me beyond our usual banter. I baited him about his ongoing joblessness, his refusal to get on with life at age thirty-two. Whether I was witty or cruel or both, he responded with the same good humor, as though he were simply glad to be spending time with me after the long separations of the past decade.

"I don't know, Zwieb. For almost five years I worked hard in the service of my country. I figure I deserve some time off."

"It's been almost a year."

"What about my job at Channel Four?"

"That lasted—what? Three months?"

"Three and a half. Also I worked at a few restaurants."

"Just can't find the right venue?"

He laughed. "I don't know, Zwieb. When you've worked in the business as long as I have"—he said this as though he'd managed a string of renowned bistros in Provence— "you get picky. I just can't stand being around fuckups."

"And yet it may shock you to learn that there are those who consider *you* a fuckup."

Still he laughed, which emboldened me to widen my field of attack. I began to recount every lurid highlight from his long career: the arrests, the car wrecks, the lost jobs, the drugs, on and on. "That was a long time ago," he'd say, or "That car was a piece of shit anyway," or "What? You've never been fired before?" or "What? You've never smoked a little pot?"

"Scott!" I said finally, throwing my hands up with a wondering laugh. "Face it! You're a disgrace!"

His face mottled a little, but he looked thoughtful. "I don't think that's true," he said. "I think I'm a very nice person. I'm just not—" He paused, searching the rafters for the right phrase; then he smiled. "I'm just not conventionally ambitious."

Later we went back to our room, where we could indulge in more serious drinking out of the public eye. While I lay on the bed and soaked, skimming a book or magazine, Scott sat on the floor and railed at the TV.

"Knocker down and piss on her! . . . You know what you *look* like? You have any idea? . . . Fuck . . . Piece a shit. What a mind-blowing piece a shit . . . Admit it! You're a fucking lesbian! And you! *Faggot* . . . Right, like I'm gonna buy your fucking beer cause your *tits* are so big . . ."

Some of this was meant to amuse me, I guess, but most of it was so much oblivious ranting. It occurred to me that this was how Scott spent his days: getting sloshed and talking to himself, or rather the TV, which I suppose served as a surrogate for the world he'd rejected and vice versa. It was a very depressing spectacle. I tried not to look or listen, but this was impossible of course, and I found myself becoming angry—angry at my father for conceiving this little get-together in the first place, for putting me in a single room with my crazy brother; angry at my brother for being so noisily, depressingly crazy; angry at my stepfamily for everything. I wanted to dash my brains out against the wall.

Finally I had to get out, but there was no shaking Scott. He thought I was enjoying the whole binge as much as he, and it might have been risky to disabuse him: much of his weird anger at the TV, I realized, was by way of blowing off steam after the beating he'd taken at lunch. So we went bar-hopping. And since I couldn't bear to hear him talk, I talked about myself. Scott was a good listener: he nodded a lot, his eyes welling up when I began sobbing about my ex-girlfriend Kate who never wrote me anymore, and we seemed to agree that the world was a pretty fucked-up place. My last memory of that night was Scott holding me upright while I puked in the snow.

The next morning our father let himself into our room—we'd failed to appear at breakfast—and found us passed out amid a reek of liquor and vomit. Wearily he told us to get packed and ready to go within an hour, and hardly spoke during the long drive back to Oklahoma. (Sandra and her children stayed in Santa Fe to enjoy the rest of the vacation.) In the car I read aloud from Joseph Mitchell's *Up in the Old Hotel*, my Christmas gift to our father. Scott especially enjoyed "Professor Seagull," Mitchell's profile of the Greenwich Village bohemian Joe Gould, a Harvard graduate who'd led a skid-row life as a matter of choice. Scott let go with a lot of wild, wheezy laughter and I joined him, what the hell, as if Gould reminded us, amusingly, of our mutual disgrace.

THERE WAS NO question of my seeing Sandra and her kids after that, and eventually Burck dropped me too—worn down by the daily grind of Sandra's subtle and not-so-subtle persuasion to the effect that I was a worthless character. That I was sane and sober enough to hold a responsible job—I'd been hired as a teacher of gifted students at a good magnet school—didn't cut much ice. Actually there had been one more Christmas, a year later, when I'd spent a single evening in my father's company; Sandra and her children had already departed for Santa Fe, minus the Bailey men, leaving me a chirpy card lest I take their absence amiss. My father, in a grim mood, informed me of their misgivings in a way that let me know he emphatically shared them, and afterward sent me the following note: "You are a very serious alcoholic. You will disagree. I am right; you are wrong." I replied in a spirit of jaunty demurral, and that tore it. We hardly spoke for the next five years.

Sandra wanted me out of the picture, and now she had her wish. As a matter of recompense, perhaps, she renewed her efforts to be a bountiful stepmother to Scott. It came as no surprise that he was invited, and I was not, to our father's lavish sixtieth birthday party, held at the ranch in Chandler, Oklahoma—Breeze Hill—that he'd bought a few months before. Scott's date was Maryam, the crazy girlfriend who'd phoned me in New Orleans and threatened suicide. She made a lasting impression by never once letting go of Scott's arm.

Scott needed all the support he could get. More than a year had passed since he'd lost his job at the TV station, and he seemed less and less apt to do anything about it. "I live the life I love, and I love the life I live," he liked to say, sighing into a comfy old recliner in front of his TV. He was living off a VA disability pension of roughly five hundred dollars a month (for an injured neck and related back problems) as well as handouts from our parents; he was also amassing a lot of credit-card debt, which explained the elaborate stereo system and brand-new desk in his study, where he claimed to make extra cash as a freelance copy-editor. Up to a point, his serene acceptance of his own inertia was convincing: he liked the little house that he "rented" from our father, and the fact that he wasn't "conventionally ambitious" became a point of oft-repeated pride. He also found comfort in Maryam, to say nothing of their churchgoing (they both attended Crossroads). More than ever he affected a kind of smug disapproval over the fact that I wasn't "saved," particularly when I tried to needle him about his lazy, aimless life.

I doubted he had the inner resources to keep it up. He was an intelligent person who'd never bothered to cultivate intelligent tastes. His life had shrunk around three basic interests: pop music, peckerwood religion, and the Dallas Cowboys. (The last was a great passion of his childhood, and now, in his mid-thirties, Exley-like, he again spent autumn weekdays pining for the excitement of Sunday afternoon.) Naturally it took more and more stimulants to persuade Scott that life held something good in store. When drunk or high, he doubtless took refuge in the same old fantasies: I picture him prancing around his house naked, the stereo booming, his bottle a makeshift microphone as he imagines a sea of pubescent fans. Meanwhile his old friends had moved on with their lives—even Todd the Tortoise had started a family and gotten a steady job. Chance meetings with such people were an awful ordeal: "Freelance stuff," Scott would mumble when asked what he was "doing" these days, and his oily face would burn with humiliation.

His only true remaining friend (that I knew of) was a skinny guy with a goatee named Thomas, who played in a western swing band and spoke French. By the time I met Thomas, I'd heard all about him: my mother dropped his name as a good angel in Scott's life, as proof that Scott was still worthy of "interesting" friends, and even my father deemed Thomas "a nice enough guy" (the latter's band played at his sixtieth birthday party). I liked Thomas all right. He was a little too carefully articulate—out of proportion, I thought, to his actual intellect—and had a tendency to romanticize my brother as a brilliant quirky fellow who couldn't be satisfied by ordinary occupations. Thomas supported himself by waiting tables at an upscale restaurant; he was the one who'd gotten Scott those short-lived waiting jobs that he'd mentioned during our lunch in Santa Fe. Thomas seemed to admire my brother's integrity for refusing to work with people he didn't respect.

Over the holidays Scott insisted I come along to a club where Thomas's band was playing, and when I heard how good they were, and said so, Scott looked very pleased—as if his own life had been vindicated by proxy. But the most notable thing about that night was meeting Andrea. I picked her up: from our balcony table I saw her standing near the stage, alone, short and a little too fleshy, with long disorderly hair and (I noticed on closer inspection) a slight overbite. But the overall effect was strangely appealing. Tipsily I took her hand and led her back to our table without a word. Turned out she was an old friend of Thomas, home for Christmas; the rest of the year she lived in Seattle. For some reason we got to talking about Russian literature, and I happened to mention Nabokov's concept of *poshlost* (philistine vulgarity). Andrea was impressed, and later we went back to Scott's house and screwed in his bed.

To Andrea I remained the guy who talked about *poshlost*. That spring she moved back to Oklahoma City and became Thomas's (platonic) roommate, and hence Scott's companion as well. Meanwhile she wrote me a lot of long, carefully articulate letters, the most common theme of which was my brother's bad behavior.

Among other things she told me that Scott called her almost every night, drunk, and invariably became abusive ("fucking whore," etc); then, just as invariably, he'd call her the next day and apologize. Also she reported that their friend Thomas wasn't quite the good angel Marlies had figured him to be. According to Andrea he drank a fifth of bourbon every night, sometimes crouching by his bedroom window with a loaded shotgun.

By the time I saw Andrea again, the following summer, she'd moved back to her mother's house, and no wonder: among the first things I noticed there, in the kitchen, was a heavy marble table with a ragged crack down the middle, as if it had been roughly toppled to the floor. Somehow I knew this was the work of either Scott or Thomas, her two great friends.

"Scott or Thomas?" I asked.

"Scott," she replied.

EVER SINCE SCOTT'S discharge from the marines he and Marlies had been making each other miserable (*more* miserable, I mean). Over the years Burck had adopted a tolerant, kindly, only somewhat deploring attitude toward Scott, while my mother had become all the more brazen. When she and Scott were together it was just a matter of time before they went from cooing and canoodling—there was always a lot of that—to a hideous crescendo of bilingual abuse. I kept advising my mother to practice Buddha-like detachment, to give up hope in other words, or at least (like Burck) let go of her headier illusions. But she was incapable of this. "He was a wonderful marine!" she'd say, or "If only he could stop *drinking*"—this when called upon to defend him. At other times she'd look weary, haunted, and say, "Ah God, what have I *wrought?*"

That Christmas I remember standing in the kitchen with Marlies as we listened to Scott (in the other room) opening his first beer of the morning; I could picture his petulant concentration as he poured. "This is going to be awful," my mother sighed. "Families are the devil's work!" I told her to relax and let him drink; with any luck he'd pass out early. Such were our hopes for a happy holiday.

But Scott was in good fettle. We sang carols at the piano while our mother cooked, and I was glad to hear that Scott had finally stopped trying to sing like Robert Plant—perhaps he'd noticed that his own voice was pretty bad, and hence put the worst of his rock-star dreams to rest. Later we opened presents, and Scott and I were both pleased with what we'd gotten each other. I'd splurged on a hefty tome titled *75 Seasons: The Complete Story of the National Football League*, with the great Cowboy halfback Emmitt Smith on the cover. "*Zwiiieeeb*," Scott sighed happily, skimming the pictures, casting ahead to the happy hours he'd fill this way. "This is *exactly* what I wanted." (So Marlies had told me.) He closed the book, clasped it to his bosom, and kissed me on the cheek—a poignant reminder of the unself-conscious way we used to kiss as children. Scott's gift to me was no less apt: a CD of Elvis's Christmas hits (I dig Elvis), the jacket a snowy pop-up Graceland. We sat on the floor and sang "Blue Christmas" together, or rather I sang while my brother provided the Jordanaires backup ("*oo-ooo-oo-ooo-oo*"). A photo of that moment is my second favorite of Scott and me.

I PRESSED MY luck with another meeting a few days later. We met at his place, and for some reason the little house was especially grim that day: furnished with the stuff of our childhood—the cheap foam-cushioned sofas and wooden stools (in storage all these years) that we'd had when our father was an ill-paid prosecutor in the AG's office. A kind of gloomy museum. The paneled walls were mostly bare. In the study was an old portrait of Scott and me, ages twelve and nine, taken at a studio in Vinita (Scott looks jaunty with the knowledge that he's still more handsome than I).

It wasn't a place I could bear in the pearly winter sunlight of 3:00 P.M.—so off we went, the drinks on me. What I remember most about that afternoon was the way we kept getting cut off at every bar, usually after the first drink. I hadn't been cut off since my college days, and only then in the wee hours when I could hardly balance myself on a stool. But strangers, especially bartenders, were able to see Scott more objectively than I: they knew at a glance he was bad news. And Scott was mostly stoical about this, as though he'd gotten used to it by now. Once—we'd been cut off again, the third or fourth time, and had promised to leave as soon as we finished our pool game—he sized up a shot and said, with a low chuckle, "I know there's something fucked up about me, Zwieb." It was the only time I can ever remember his admitting as much.

Finally we were both so drunk there was no question of being served anywhere. Hungry, we stopped at a seedy takeout place on our way back to Scott's house. While we sat in a booth waiting for our order, I lapsed into a crying jag, rather like the one I'd had in Santa Fe. The nominal reason was my father's desertion of me, and Scott was as sympathetic as ever: he assured me that Papa would come to his senses, and said the usual hard things about Sandra. He stroked my head and dabbed at my cheeks with a paper napkin. The fact was, I wouldn't have cried, then or before, if not for Scott's presence: the prospect of a night in his company, in that hopeless little house, was crushing.

And yet I hadn't foreseen the worst. After a few french fries

I passed out on Scott's sofa—or rather I fell into a kind of pre-liminary stupor wherein I was just conscious enough to notice a tongue in my mouth that wasn't my own, yet dazed enough to think this might be a good thing. Perhaps it was Scott's breath (tainted with beer and fried food) that brought me up short. I shook my head and pushed. Sitting up, I saw Scott return to his chair.

"Were you *kissing* me?"

He shrugged. "It's no big deal."

I didn't know what to say. I made a show of eating my food.

"You want a beer?" Scott asked. He was watching TV now.

"No, thanks. I'd better get going actually."

"Sure you can drive?"

"Oh yeah. I'm not that drunk anymore really."

Outside I had to walk in front of Scott's living room window on the way to my car. I couldn't resist a glance inside: he was staring at the TV with owlish concentration, but stiffly flourished a hand as I passed.

part IV

stille nacht

A year later Scott was in a medium-security prison. The one time I visited, he went on about the lawsuit he was bringing against the Oklahoma City Police and Department of Corrections. "*That's* going into my lawsuit!" he liked to say, calling himself "the white Rodney King." His own quixotic posturing seemed to amuse him (ditto my mother, in a different way perhaps), while at the same time he seemed quite serious.

Things had fallen apart a few months after our good Christmas in 1994, at a time when my parents were relatively hopeful. Scott had decided to go back to school. He seemed to realize that he'd never get a decent job without a college degree, and by "decent job" he meant something interesting and exotic, not a mundane compromise like the marines. He planned to major in music and become a record producer. He was picky about schools, too. He refused to attend community college and was "too old" for a vo-tech like the Drahn School of Business; however, his failure to last a full semester in two previous tries at four-year colleges made a third try problematic. Fortunately our father knew someone on the board of trustees at Oklahoma City University, and after a certain amount of haggling he was able to arrange Scott's enrollment for the fall 1995 semester.

Scott seemed excited, full of plans. When I saw him that summer he showed me a mahogany lectern he'd bought on credit so he could do his homework standing up, because of his bad back. Well in advance, too, he'd gotten a number of textbooks for his classes on musical theory and the like, along with some noncurricular material about the record business. But it also seemed to depress him, vaguely, that by the time he graduated he'd be pushing forty, and not-so-deep down he doubted he'd graduate at all.

"What about the time I . . . ?" he'd say to our friend Andrea, whenever she tried to encourage him. Because she went out of her way to seem unshocked by the many disasters of his life, Scott compulsively told her the worst, the better to talk her out of having faith in him. "But you're so *smart*," she'd say, or "That was a long time ago. Put it behind you. It's never too late to start over." And Scott would nod—receptively, pensively—then say, "But what about . . . ?"

The bad news came in late August, a few days before Scott's classes were scheduled to begin. My mother's old boyfriend, Dave, called me in New Orleans.

"I think you'd better sit down," he said. "There's been an accident."

For a terrible moment I thought he was talking about my

mother, who at the time was visiting friends on Long Island. Then I thought he meant my father, worse still, since we'd yet to reconcile; in Marlies's absence it made sense that Dave would be the first to bring news, since at the time I doubted even tragedy could compel Sandra to call me.

"Your brother had a car wreck."

This was something of an anticlimax, given what I'd been hearing from Andrea, and I remember feeling miffed at Dave for that melodramatic "you'd better sit down."

"Really? Is he dead, or what?"

He wasn't dead. The rather wacky facts of the case were these: Scott had managed to re-create (and improve on) his colossal smash-up of the Cadillac fourteen years before—that is, he'd lost control on an exit ramp and driven almost head-on into a concrete embankment (no mere guardrail this time). Had he been driving his old BMW, he would have been killed instantly; but his BMW was in the shop. He'd finally gotten around to having it painted, also on credit. As for the rental he drove—at suicidal speed, stone drunk—it was a late-model Ford and therefore had an air bag, which saved his life.

Dave noted, however, that Scott might have some brain damage. "The bag hit his head pretty hard. His face looks like he fell asleep on a waffle iron."

"Is he conscious?"

"Yes and no. He talks, but he doesn't make much sense. Repeats himself a lot. You know, his short-term memory is shot."

"You told Mom?"

"Oh yes." Dave allowed himself a chuckle. "You can imagine: 'That asshole! He can *rot* in the hospital for all I care!' Etcetera, etcetera."

"Did she say *Unkraut vergeht nicht?*"

"In so many words."

But when I spoke to my mother that night, she seemed drained of her usual bluster. She'd been having such a good time on Long Island; it made sense that Scott would spoil it.

"Pam's children are so sweet and *normal*," she said.

Pam was her American "sister," part of a nice Port Washington family that had taken care of my mother as a wayward nineteen-year-old, newly arrived from Germany. Pam, like her parents, was nothing if not conventionally middle class, conventionally decent, and so represented a sort of Road Not Taken in Marlies's life. Once or twice in New York I'd met Pam's children—two grown daughters and a son—and I can vouch for the fact that they're all likable, handsome young people with good jobs.

"Such beautiful manners!" said my mother. "I mean they wait on me hand and foot. 'You need another drink, Marlies?' 'Here, take my chair.' That sort of thing." She sighed. "Even before I heard of this latest . . . *shit* with Scott, I was thinking how nice it would be to have kids like that." I was about to point out the invidious implications of that remark when she added, "I mean can you imagine Frank calling his mother a *cunt*?"

Frank was Pam's son, and I certainly couldn't imagine him calling his mother—or any woman, ever—a cunt. At the same time I couldn't imagine Pam saying any number of things that Marlies was apt to say on a routine basis, and I was tempted to suggest as much. But I let it go.

"If only Scott could stop *drinking*," I said with only moderate sarcasm, "he'd be just as nice a boy as Frank."

"Bullshit!" my mother replied, and when I asked whether she planned to cut her vacation short and see about Scott, she was even more adamant: "Hell no! That asshole! He can *rot* in the hospital for all I care . . ."

I felt reassured by this return to form. If Scott's latest mishap had the effect of waking my mother up, of distancing her from Scott's awful life, then it was a good thing.

AFTER A WEEK or so, the worst effects of Scott's head injury had worn off, and he began calling me on the phone. His voice was a bit slurred and he still repeated himself a lot, but he was coherent enough. What he mainly lacked was the capacity to censor himself, to sift the truth as we all must (alcoholics and drug addicts especially) in order to put forth an acceptable public self. I didn't listen very carefully, but what I heard was pretty sordid: he missed drugs the way a glutton missed snacks, and spoke in rhapsodic detail about freebasing and needles and so forth; he said a lot about sex that I simply tuned out. Andrea—who often called with updates I didn't particularly want—was glad to remind me of anything I might have missed. For example, she assured me that Scott had hustled his body for drugs, quite a bit in fact, and quoted him as follows: "'They have something you want, you have something they want.'" I tried not to imagine the kind of people who'd barter drugs to fuck my brother.

Later Scott denied all this—certainly he didn't remember saying it—but there was no denying what was found in his house. There were dildos of every conceivable size, shape, and color: double-dicked, stubbled, strapped, gargantuan, wan, uncircumsized, black, white, yellow. And then there were my brother's crack stems, twenty or so, all of them blackened with use. There was also a small box of photos: Scott, nude, striking a number of homoerotic poses—e.g., leering over his shoulder with comic salacity while he thrusts his buttocks toward the camera and spreads his cheeks for a good view of his anus. Years later my mother showed me these and couldn't help giggling: "What an old *sow!*"

It was Sandra who discovered that last item—for *that* I would have liked to be a fly on the wall. She and my father had decided to evict Scott while he was still in the hospital, and Dave was good enough to help her box up his things and haul them back to a storage shed at my mother's place. ("Let this be a lesson to all of us," Dave said afterward. "Make sure you hide your dildos and crack pipes before you take off on a drunk-driving spree.") I'd always assumed such lurid artifacts were the main reason Burck and Sandra had decided to banish Scott for good, and I considered this rather rash and bigoted, all the more so in view of my bitterness toward them at the time. Scott was sick: what he needed was a nice mental hospital where he could watch TV in a haze of medication; more to be pitied than censured.

But, according to Andrea, my father couldn't have been more callous. "If you call me here *one more time,*" he said to Scott (as Andrea told it), when the latter persisted in ringing his office from the hospital, "I'm gonna have the DA come down there and drag your sorry ass away in leg irons." Andrea's version of events seemed contrived to persuade me that my kindly, liberal-minded father had reverted at last to a mean old Babbitt: *poshlost.*

But this was not the whole story, as I learned some years later, during one of my rapprochements with Burck.

"I think it was the head injury that did him in," he remarked one day, as we sat by a pond at his ranch with Jack, Sandra's Australian Cattle Dog. "When we visited Scott at the hospital—"

"You guys went to the hospital?"

He gave me a puzzled look. "Well, of course we did. We were worried about him. But he was just"—my father winced at the muddy water, shaking his head—"*repulsive.* Worse than I'd ever seen him, and I thought I'd seen the worst. He yelled at the nurses like I wouldn't yell at *Jack*. His language was beyond disgusting. Beyond abusive. Finally he said something to Sandra that I—well, that was just *it* as far as I was concerned. That was it."

He coughed, then abruptly bent over in his chair and clapped his hands. "C'mere, Jack! C'mere, boy!" The dog panted and gamboled at his feet.

IT WAS TRUE Scott wasn't a model patient at the hospital. He constantly complained about pain—indeed had suffered a certain amount of trauma to his neck and other parts, never mind his head—and was duly medicated, which snuffed whatever remained of his inhibitions. He staggered around the halls, bellowing, more or less in the nude, whenever he sensed the nurses were neglecting him. He badgered other patients too. Finally (so said Andrea), he and Maryam were caught screwing in his bed, and maybe that's what led to his expulsion—either that or indigence, once my father made it clear he didn't intend to pay Scott's bills anymore.

On the day of his removal I got a call from his friend Thomas, who said a lot of indignant things about my parents' refusal to get involved. He assumed I'd be an ally.

"He's their fucking *son*, man! And now they're fucking him same as they did you!"

"Well, in Scott's case—"

"You know where he is now?"

"Where?"

"He's sitting in a fucking *wheel*chair in the parking lot, nowhere to go. Andrea and I just *now* had to tell him he doesn't have a house anymore."

"How'd he take it?"

"Not well."

"Did he mention the dildos and crack pipes?"

"The what?"

"Look. I'm sorry about this, but I'm not sure what you want me to—"

What Thomas wanted me to do was call my father and find out where Scott's birth certificate and service papers were, so they could get him admitted to the VA. Thomas himself had tried calling the ranch, but Sandra was put off by his tone and hung up on him; now she wasn't answering at all. It was a weekend, and she always screened my father's calls on the weekend. I hadn't spoken to either of them in over a year and was, if anything, more likely to be screened than Thomas. Nevertheless I felt obliged to try.

"Hi, folks," I said, when the machine beeped, "sorry to bother you. I was just wondering if you had any idea—"

Sandra picked up and greeted me with a kind of no-hard-feelings civility: what could she do for me? What indeed. I knew it was pointless to ask for my father. I explained about Scott.

"I see. Well, as I tried to tell Thomas, we don't have anything like that. Maybe your mother . . . ?"

I sighed. My mother was the one who'd advised Thomas to call Sandra and my father in the first place (*not*, I suspect, because she thought they had Scott's papers, but because she wanted them to suffer equally).

"I'll give it a try," I said. "Well. Nice talking to you, Sandra. Say hi to Papa for me."

"I will!"

I waited for Thomas to call me back.

"What'd they say?"

"They don't have his papers."

"Fuck!"

"You could take him to your place."

"He needs a *hospital*, man! If your fucking parents—"

"Lay off my parents. They've been putting up with this shit for twenty years. You want my advice? Walk away. Leave him in the parking lot. Maybe someone will come along and roll him somewhere nice."

This silenced Thomas for a moment or two; then he said something loud and nasty and hung up. I was glad to be rid of him, and I didn't hear from him again for a long time. Andrea was a different matter. For a number of weeks she kept leaving updates on my answering machine: Scott was in the VA; Scott was thrown out of the VA; Scott had broken into her house and stolen something; Scott was HIV positive, or so she'd heard (from whom?). Often she called simply in the hope that I'd pick up—her silences on my machine had a kind of identifiably needy quality—but I vowed never to answer my phone until I was quite sure she'd stopped calling for good. Finally she moved back to Seattle, or so I later heard.

ONCE, YEARS BEFORE all this, when Scott and I were drinking together—his life had just turned to shit for the umpteenth time—he got sort of a gloating look and said:

"Ma will never give up on me."

In this respect he was more prescient than I. After he'd smashed up the rental car and given himself brain damage, after his dildos and crack stems and sundry erotica had been discovered, I actually believed my mother when she told me she was *through* with that asshole, he could *rot* in the hospital, etc. About a month later, though, he was living with her.

"*What could I do?*" she said in a frenzied way when I upbraided her. "He looks so emaciated! His skin is gray! He'll *die* if I don't help him!"

"Let him die!"

"Don't say that. You don't mean that."

"*Let him die.* Better him than you!"

But she wouldn't let him die. It helped Scott's cause that she was particularly vulnerable at the time: after fifteen years under the same roof, Dave the boyfriend had just moved out; he was a lot younger than she and wanted a proper wife and kids; besides, they were driving each other crazy. But Marlies wasn't ready to be alone yet, and after a fashion she still loved Dave, a decent guy whose eagerness to leave had shaken her badly. So I suppose Scott performed a service of sorts—namely he managed to persuade her (at least temporarily) that there were worse things than being alone.

Indeed, she was so traumatized by Scott's presence that she later claimed to have no memory of his stay, though I remember what she told me at the time. Nothing very dramatic happened. Scott convalesced on the couch, quietly, and barely seemed to notice our mother. He never went anywhere because there was nowhere to go. A big supply of pain pills and whatever else obviated the one errand he was liable to run. He got up only to go to the bathroom, and seemed content to lie there forever as long as certain needs were met.

Marlies couldn't take it. Scott seemed a waxen embodiment of everything that had gone wrong in her life. After a week or so, she asked him to leave.

"Why?" he asked, vaguely hurt.

"You're just too depressing, Scott."

"Why?"

"Go to the hospital! You need help!"

"There's nothing wrong with *me*."

But finally he left. As long as his things were in my mother's storage shed, and she provided his only permanent address and therefore received his mail (unpaid bills, the usual magazines, his monthly VA check, and free motivational tapes and assorted literature with titles like "15 Minutes That Will Change Your Life!"), he knew he had plenty of reasons for returning.

One day he showed up asking for money. He needed a hundred bucks to tide him over for the rest of the month, and since he already owed Marlies a great deal of money and seemed to accept that she wouldn't give him more until he'd made some effort to lessen his debt, he offered to write her a postdated check. He mentioned with a kind of pride that he was cutting corners by living out of his car, the newly painted BMW; in fact the hundred dollars was needed for minor repairs. It was an old car.

He spoke in a kind of rapid monotone, as though he'd rehearsed the spiel a thousand times and was eager to get it over with. His eyes seemed to stare past my mother to the money and whatever he wanted to buy with it. She knew he wasn't leaving without a hundred dollars, and the main thing was to make him leave. She'd have to get cash at an ATM, she said, and suggested he wait, have a snack, but he preferred to follow her in his car.

From my mother's place in the country to the nearest ATM was maybe ten miles, and never once was Scott more than a few feet from my mother's bumper. The roar of his stereo made it all the more menacing, like being overtaken by a tsunami. At stoplights my mother shook her fist at Scott in the rearview mirror, mouthed obscenities, appealed to his belief in a benevolent deity, but each time she was met with the same blankly determined stare. Finally they arrived at the ATM. My mother got the money, parked, and bustled over to where my brother sat in his BMW.

"Are you out of your *mind*? Are you trying to get us *killed*?"

Scott pondered this. "I guess I'm just a crazy motherfucker," he said.

"*Look at yourself!*" She reached into his car and adjusted the rearview mirror; Scott obliged her by staring at himself, cocking his head with old fondness. "You need help! Go to the VA!"

He lowered his eyes and sighed. "You're right. I will."

"You can't go *on* like this!"

"I know. You're right."

She gave him the money. "Promise?"

He nodded like a little boy about to cry. She kissed his cheek—too sallow even to support pimples—and asked him to call her later.

A couple of weeks later he called her from the county jail. I never got the story straight, but what happened went something like this: the police found Scott sleeping in his car outside a crack house; there were drugs in the car, etc. Things might have gone better if Scott had seen fit to cooperate with the police, but I gather he resisted, strenuously, and was eventually sentenced to five years in prison. Somewhere in there his postdated check to my mother bounced.

SHORTLY AFTER SCOTT'S arrest my mother had sent me his mug shot: he looked like a surly pillar of oatmeal, a scraggly beard thrown in for whimsical effect. I wanted nothing to do with that person ever again, though I wished him no ill. I was glad to know he'd get three squares a day and be kept out of mischief, more or less.

And really, even if he weren't in prison, I would have still been inclined to phase him out of my life. At thirty-two I was finally getting my shit together, a process expedited when I met my future wife, Mary, then an undergraduate at the University of Chicago. She was home on one of those weird trimester holidays, and had rollerbladed to the school where I taught to pick up her little sister's homework assignments. This was during my planning period, so I had time to flirt with her—*quite* taken with this tall, sweaty, self-possessed young woman who was the older sister of Emma, a sweet but rather farouche thirteen-year-old who'd just broken her leg. In Mary I sensed a slight, kindred shyness, and I was touched by the thought of Emma growing up (as indeed she would) to become the same sort of charming, carefully composed person. I made a mental note to ask the older sister out on a date if I ever saw her again, and by one of those flukes that serve to remind one that the cosmos isn't entirely malign, I did: at a gallery opening maybe four months later. We were both glad to see each other. Chatting, Mary mentioned that she was a teacher's aide at a public school in Chicago—part of her work scholarship at the university—and also helped a teacher friend at an elementary school in the French Quarter. Casting about, I invited her to guest-teach one of my gifted classes, after which I took her out for drinks, and we went on from there.

I'll never forget the day I knew, for certain, that this was the one person I absolutely needed in my life. We were in the Quarter and Mary suggested a quick visit to the second-grade classroom at McDonogh 15 where she occasionally helped out. Her reception there was something to see: all twenty or so kids, in unison, rose screeching to their feet and flung themselves at Mary as though she were covered in honey or dollar bills. The uproar continued for two or three minutes—Mary, struggling to keep her feet, was buffeted around like a bell buoy in a rough sea—until the teacher, Bonnie, demanded the kids desist already so they could get on with their lesson. She was otherwise undismayed; Mary's goodness, apparently, always had that effect. Kids and dogs know.

The following summer Mary spent most nights at my apartment, and I came to realize the extent to which my drinking had been a matter of simple, lonely boredom. At any rate Mary didn't drink much, and for her sake I dispensed with all but a single nightly martini. It was strange to feel good in the morning again; it occurred to me that for almost ten years I'd taken for granted a kind of incidental crapulence. Also it was good not to feel like such an impostor. Nowadays when people said nice things about me as a teacher and so on, I felt less of an urge to laugh. And how nice, how companionable it was to cook a meal in my kitchen, looking up now and then to see the back of Mary's head as she lay reading on my couch. This was how one lived.

EVERY MONTH OR so I'd get a letter from Scott. He never wrote of his immediate circumstances, except to repeat the phrase "I hate this fucking place" every few paragraphs. I got the impression the letters were scribbled in the midst of a bottomless ennui, and might have been scribbled to anybody. I'd scan the pages for any sign of a personal reference, any hint of shared history, but other than the odd snide remark about Burck or Sandra, there was nothing but random chatter about magazines, starlets, sports, Jesus, and various cars he coveted (the new Porsche Boxster was a special favorite). And hyphens: always the envelope bulged with newspaper clippings marked up with deleted or inserted hyphens, which Scott thought were subject to a veritable pandemic of misuse. He was immune to remonstrance on this point. Perhaps he thought it called attention to his acumen as a copy-editor, one of the few creditable aspects of his life prior to prison.

For the first year or so of his sentence Scott had been in a minimum-security facility. He was even allowed to teach some sort of literacy course, since it didn't go unnoticed that he read a lot (magazines and library books relating to his lawsuit) and had a way with words. More often than not, though, his glibness got him into trouble: it was hard to say who hated him more, the guards or the inmates; in any case he got a lot of write-ups, and finally someone set his hair on fire while he was sleeping. After that he was transferred to the medium-security prison where my mother and I paid him a visit.

It was a grim place. We stood in a little holding cage outside the walls while we were identified with a video camera; then, after a thorough frisking, we were conducted to a dingy cafeteria where inmates met their families on visiting days. Marlies had packed an elaborate lunch, and we filled the empty minutes opening various Tupperware containers and filling our plates just so. Then we sat in the flyblown heat and waited. Finally he showed up with a mass of other inmates who dispersed themselves among tables of loved ones.

Scott gave me a rough hug, pressing my head against his bony muscular chest. "*Zwiiieeeb,* look at you!" he said, surveying me at arm's length. "My God, I think he's almost pretty as me!"

Sitting down to our food, my mother remarked of Scott (as though he were absent or deaf), "I don't think he's so pretty anymore. What do you think?"

Her tone implied that the point was at least debatable and it was up to me to resolve it one way or the other. I looked at Scott— chewing, undismayed, awaiting my verdict for better or worse.

"He looks okay to me," I said. "All things considered."

"See?" said Scott. "Forever young."

He went on eating in his old way of endless fastidious nibbling, sometimes removing a piece of masticated fat to a side plate. My mother clucked and fussed at him the way *her* mother (whom she now resembled almost to a nicety) had done years before in Germany, so I imagine. I noticed Scott was balding around the temples and getting thin on top too, or perhaps that was where he'd been set on fire. The middle of his forehead was scored with jagged little creases that I thought at first were acne scars, until Scott told me they were from head-butts.

After lunch we were herded outside, where we could sit at picnic tables or wander the lawn. Somehow we got hold of a half-inflated football and chucked it around a bit, talking about the Cowboys and Redskins. Then we joined our mother at one of the shaded tables. She watched our conversation in an abstracted way, as though she were trying to picture us as children. For a while Scott talked of nothing but his lawsuit—in that half-joking, deadly serious way of his—then abruptly dropped the subject and focused on me. He wanted to know every detail of my life, or as many as I could provide in the half hour left to us: How did I meet my girlfriend? Did we sleep together on the first date? How much did I make as a teacher? Was it hard to get certified? What kind of car was I driving?

Then it was time to go.

"Well, Zwieb—"

"Well—"

And he gathered me into his arms, whacking my back a bit too hard as he let go. He didn't let go of my mother for a long time; he'd started crying and didn't want others to see. Finally he wiped his eyes against her shoulder, one and then the other, and whispered good-bye with a little gasp. On the other side of the locking

Plexiglas door we turned one more time to wave at my brother, who managed a jaunty smile as he stood bobbing slightly on the balls of his feet.

I TRIED HARDER to stay in touch with Scott after that. It pleased me to imagine him reading my letters and bursting into elaborate wheezy laughter from time to time. I sent him a few books too, until I learned that these were all confiscated pending his release. I wanted to make his life a little more bearable. I figured he'd keep getting write-ups from guards and beatings from prisoners, until it became clear that he was unwell and belonged in a mental hospital. I figured such a process was automatic for the obvious head cases. Also there was this: Scott wasn't HIV positive, apparently, but he did have hepatitis C, and would almost surely perish from liver failure if he ever got out of prison and started drinking again. It was a win-win situation as far as I was concerned, since I still believed that Scott was better off dead, though a comfortable nuthouse would do just as well.

For a while my mother seemed to agree with me, but then she returned to certain insidious phrases about his being a good marine and so on.

"Forget about the marines," I'd tell her. "He's not in the marines anymore."

"If Scott didn't drink so much—"

"He'd be a *sober* lunatic, the way he is now. He keeps sending me piles of clippings with the hyphens corrected! I tell him to stop and he only sends more! What do you call *that*?"

Which usually silenced my mother, since she got the clippings too. Nevertheless I could tell she was gradually persuading herself that Scott would benefit from another chance, that he might still do something great or at least interesting with his life. We fought bitterly about it. It was like trying to talk a drunk into giving up her car keys.

"You're as crazy as he is!" I'd end up shouting at her. "What'll it *take* with you? How many more dildos and crack pipes and car wrecks do you *need*? How many more *years* of it? Ever tell you about the time he put his *tongue* down my throat? He's sick! He's sick! He *belongs* in jail!"

My mother, usually so formidable in argument, would spar with me as best she could and then dwindle into silence or tears; her case was weak and she knew it. Finally she avoided the subject entirely. One day, though, she mentioned in passing that Scott would soon be eligible for parole.

"That can't happen," I said.

She sighed. "You're probably right."

"No 'probably' about it. It can't happen. You can't let it happen."

"What can *I* do?"

Maybe ten days later she called again.

"Guess who's here?" she said abruptly, with forced cheer.

Mary and I had been laughing on the couch when the phone rang; whatever happened to my face after "Guess who's here?" alarmed her: Had somebody died?

"That's right!" said my mother, though I hadn't said a word. "He's right here! You want to speak to him?"

"No."

"Here he is!"

". . . Zwieb?"

In the midst of my dizzy epiphany—but of *course* this was going to happen—I couldn't muster much in the way of warmth, dissembled or otherwise. I said hi and asked what he planned to do with himself. He mentioned something about his lawsuit and

I told him he was full of shit. Just like that. I think Scott tried to laugh it off, but I made it clear I wasn't trying to be funny.

"Lawsuit," I said. "What about getting a job?"

"I might do some copy-editing. I was making damn good money there for a while, Zwieb. You have a pretty distorted idea of what my life was like."

"Even the most reprehensible people," I said, quoting one of my letters, "can't be reprehensible every minute of the day. That would require a certain effort."

He gave an edgy laugh. "Watch it, Zwieb."

"Does Papa know you're out yet?"

"*Papa*," he said. "Papa's been trying to get rid of me ever since I was seventeen."

He said this with an intensity that was supposed to be persuasive, like a bad actor reciting a silly line.

"Okay, Scott. Can I speak to Mom, please?"

He tried to talk a bit longer, to win me over, but I kept asking for our mother until he gave her the phone.

"Okay, Mom," I said. "Okay." I could barely catch my breath. "You're going to have to live with this."

"What's *that* supposed to mean?"

"It means he's crazy. It means you've got a crazy alcoholic drug addict—"

"He can't drink while he's here!" she announced decisively. "That's the deal! Two beers a day! That's it!"

"Right. You heard what he said about Papa?"

"What?"

I told her.

"Well, maybe he's right," she said.

I'd been pacing from one room to the other, back and forth, but now I sat down on the floor.

"I mean we have to have a little *faith* in him!" she was saying. "Maybe he's *not* entirely wrong! Somebody has to *believe* in him!"

I told her I'd call her back in a few days and hung up. Mary was stooped beside me patting my head, which annoyed me. She asked if I wanted to talk about it.

"Scott's out of prison," I said. "He's living with my mother. And no, I don't want to talk about it right at the moment."

THAT WAS OCTOBER 1998—Scott had just turned thirty-eight—and my mother and I spoke only a few more times between then and Christmas. We knew we'd only fight over the phone, and there was no point in that; she'd made her decision and now it would have to work out one way or the other. In letters she tried to put the best spin on things: in exchange for room and board, Scott had agreed to do chores around the place—feed animals, mow grass, weed the garden, that sort of thing—and for a few weeks, all seemed to go well. Scott was not only a hardy farmhand but a pleasant undemanding companion. At night they sat around chatting, watching TV; sometimes he gave her backrubs. I wondered in my letters how this spirit of almost ideal amity had been achieved, since I'd never known them to last five minutes without going for each other's throats. My mother replied that Scott was a new man now that he'd stopped drinking so much. Two beers a day, she insisted, and "by God he sticks to it."

More and more often, however, a minor chord was struck. One night Scott had gone to a concert and returned very late, waking my mother with a lot of crashing around in the kitchen. He was totally incoherent. But the next morning (or whenever he got out of bed), Scott had an explanation: he'd forgotten to eat the day of the concert, he said, and therefore his blood sugar was parlously low. My mother reported this without a whiff of irony; rather she invited me to share her relief. Also he began to neglect his chores. Given that he had little else to do, this seemed an almost spiteful idleness; when confronted, though, he'd only shake his head in a wondering way and remark, "Oh yeah. Sorry. Well, I'll do it tomorrow." Tomorrow, it soon transpired, meant whenever he felt like it or whenever my mother was willing to risk a fight by putting her foot down. At first she was able to keep somewhat calm by reminding herself that Scott's short-term memory wasn't what it used to be.

But at last she threw in the towel.

"It's not working out," she said when we spoke a couple of days before I came home for Christmas. That my mother would admit this, to me, meant things had gone very wrong indeed.

"What's going on?"

She mentioned his indolence and so forth. Then, more reluctantly, she admitted he was drinking again and this made things "pretty bad."

"Like what?"

"Oh, you know. Pretty bad." She gave an odd chuckle, sighed. "You can't mention this when you come here . . ."

"Mention what?"

"Promise?"

"Tell me."

The fact was, Scott had assaulted her the night before. He'd come home drunk and they'd fought as usual. Finally my mother told him to get the hell out of her house, and he laughed or affected to laugh: "You were nothing but a lonely old *cunt* before I came here," he said. He put his face in hers and invited her to hit him; at first she hesitated, but he goaded her on with a voice, a face, that was so repulsive she had to lash out; just as suddenly he rammed a knee in her groin and left her writhing on the floor.

"Call the police!" I said.

"I can't do that."

"Fine. I'll call them. Better yet, I'll kill that fucker myself."

"Don't say that. Don't talk like that. Listen, he doesn't know what he's doing. Today he didn't even remember."

"Right, and he won't remember the next time either, or the time after that, and before you know it he'll kill you. You have to get him *out* of there. *Today.*"

But she insisted we wait until Christmas was over. "And don't worry," she said. "He'll move out on his own. He doesn't want to live with me either. I'm just a 'lonely old cunt' who nags him all day and won't let him drink. Let's just try to get through Christmas, okay?" Then she told me how much she missed me and her voice broke. Only two more days, I said.

SCOTT PICKED ME up at the Oklahoma City airport, since our mother had invited some friends for lunch and had to stay home and cook. I saw him before he saw me. There in the crowded baggage area he burned with a kind of lunatic charisma—eyes wide, head bobbing, bounding around on his toes: a jaybird looking for a worm. I could picture the grainy surveillance footage later, a lighted circle around Scott—the man who went on to blow up the terminal, shoot randomly into the crowd, kill his mother and brother and himself.

He spotted me and bounded over. I dropped my bag and went limp to absorb the pummeling.

"*Zwiebathane!*" he said, after he'd set me back on my feet. Scott was at least two inches taller but not as bulky as I'd become in my thirties; one reason for his rough greetings, I always thought, was to establish that he was still the stronger of the two. Also, of course, he loved me and was low on impulse control.

While we waited for the rest of my luggage, Scott talked and talked. He told me about his hepatitis C as if for the first time, having evidently forgotten the times he'd mentioned it in his letters. He seemed perfectly at ease with it.

"... oh fuck yeah, Zwieb, in those days you used the same dirty needle for *days* at a time! Just a bunch of kids." Worldly chuckle. "I remember once Todd and I had this shit ..."

"Really?" I'd say, or "Wow" or "Hm," and when I'd hear Scott bark with sudden laughter, I'd laugh a bit too. Finally my luggage arrived. Scott plucked it off the belt and bounded toward the parking lot, talking, talking.

The roads were icy, but Scott drove his old BMW fast as ever. I clutched the armrests and watched the scenery unfurl while he jabbered away. There was the lumbering oil derrick on Airport Road, the blank pastures of I-44, abruptly giving way to an ever-changing farrago of strip malls and franchise restaurants, then pasture again as we sped (wobbling a bit on the icy exit ramp) away from I-35 into the rural hinterland east of Norman. A few years later, the singer Toby Keith would erect a sprawling mansion on some land near my mother's place, but in those days it was just trees and cattle and the odd country church, all of it jumbling past while Scott talked and talked. He'd always prided himself on his ability to maneuver under adverse conditions, and now he was taking turns at top speed with only a touch of tailspin, or coming to a slippery stop in the nick of time—talking, talking. From the moment I'd spotted Scott at the airport I was sorry I'd come, and now, thirty minutes later, I was sorrier than ever.

"... *that's* going into my lawsuit!" he proclaimed at a stoplight.

"Let's not talk about that, okay?"

It was the first thing I'd said in a while, and we were both startled by the anger in my voice.

"About what?"

"Your 'lawsuit.' "

His eyes narrowed on the road and he said, "Fine."

The talking stopped.

At last we arrived at my mother's house. While Scott skidded along the wavering gravel driveway, I was thinking how unsuitable the place was for housing a lunatic: the nearest neighbors were perhaps a quarter mile away, and the rustling woods would drown our screams.

Hearing the dogs bark, my mother came out to greet me. From a distance I thought she looked great—thinner than I'd seen her in years. Then I saw how haggard she was. By then Scott had been living with her for more than two months. She hugged me and wouldn't let go. I tried a bit of levity—"Hey, *thanks* for sending Scott to get me"—but she only clutched me harder and shook her head against my chest. "I had to *cook*," she said in a tragic voice. We walked arm-in-arm back to the house, Scott bounding ahead with my luggage.

Our guests had already arrived, an old couple named Younghein and their middle-aged daughter. My mother had met the Youngheins some thirty years ago at a "discussion group" in the suburbs; they were nice folks who made a hobby of various left-wing causes. Mrs. Younghein was the crankier of the two: when I was a kid, she'd dragged me along to an anti-nuke rally at the capitol, and nowadays her cause was the pollution associated with chicken farms. Shrunken with age and various diseases, she held forth on the subject while her husband smiled benignly. Every few minutes she'd lapse into a pettish silence and chew her food, exhausted, whereupon the daughter would start chatting about her travels. It was very dull, but I welcomed dullness after my ride with Scott.

They knew about his troubles, of course, and Scott knew they knew. Every little gesture of his was calculated with this in mind. He was elaborately well-mannered and spoke with a kind of fussy Latinate pretension (*indubitably*), alert to the effect he was having on the rest of us.

Later we sat around the living room drinking coffee and talking about the past. Scott was still at the table having a soul chat with the daughter. (Perhaps she was telling him—at my mother's behest?—about an obstacle she'd overcome in her own life.) Old Mrs. Younghein had talked herself out about chicken farms and wasn't much interested in reminiscing. She sat slumped in her chair, dazed and gloomy.

"We need to go!" she'd croak from time to time, and my mother would tell her it was early and Mr. Younghein would pat her arm in a mollifying way.

I wondered why my mother was dragging this out. Once upon a time she'd been so impatient with bores and boredom—but then so many of her colorful old friends, the funny gay men and so forth, were gone forever. Life had come full circle or something . . . or so I reflected, casting about for a talking point, when one of Scott's laughs split the air and it occurred to me that the Youngheins made my mother feel safe. Nothing very bad could happen around such dull, decent people. If nothing else Scott would put off getting drunk.

Finally, as night fell, they left. Mr. Younghein and I stood on either side of his wife and helped her totter over the gravel while the daughter gave my brother a hug and urged him to call her anytime: "I *mean* that, Scott: anytime." I waved good-bye to our guests, confident I'd never see them again, and wandered back inside to some bookshelves along the hall. I was through being sociable. I meant to grab a few of my mother's photo albums and retire to a back room to ponder our family saga.

"HEY ZWIEB."

I'd gone through a few albums and had skulked back into the hall to grab some more, when Scott (lying in wait?) rounded the corner with a large, half-empty glass of beer in his hand. Already there was a subtle change in his manner: he breathed in careful, hissing doses and stood a bit more formally than before.

"How d'you like being a teacher?"

Whenever he'd asked me this in the past, I'd always said "Fine" and added some sort of disclaimer about the pain-in-the-ass principal or pain-in-the-ass parents—this to make him feel better about lacking any professional status himself. Now I said something about the pain-in-the-ass kids, how thirteen is a difficult age and so on.

"Thirteen," Scott said huskily. He gave me a little push. "Hey Zwieb, you ever fuck one of your students?"

"No," I said.

"Man." He shook his head and sipped his beer. "Thirteen."

I excused myself and proceeded to the back room. Shut the door. Sat in the gathering dusk. After a while I turned on a lamp and realized I'd forgotten to grab more photo albums; since their retrieval would mean leaving the room and possibly bumping into Scott again, I picked up a book from the lamp table and tried to read. By now Scott and my mother were having a loud discussion in the living room; I could hear bits and pieces if I listened. Most of what Scott said, as ever when he was drunk or getting that way, was liberally sprinkled with the word "fuck" in various forms.

"Fuck that," I heard him say. "If you fucking *think* I'm getting a job, then you don't fucking know the first thing about me!"

He didn't sound particularly aggressive. Rather he seemed amused by the fact that, after all these years, our mother still didn't understand him.

"But what will you do?"

"I've always gotten by, you don't have to fucking *worry* about it."

"But I'm curious, Scott. You can't stay here forever."

"I don't need your . . ."

What I mostly noticed was the pains our mother took not to provoke him: she kept him going with ingenuous little questions and sometimes laughed at his answers, careful to make it clear she was laughing with rather than at him. After all these years she was finally afraid of him; also, I think, she wanted to keep him engaged so he wouldn't bother *me*. She wanted me to enjoy my visit.

But after a while it petered out—his chair gave a loud creak as he lurched to his feet and my mother sighed "Not another beer, Scott, *please*"—and sure enough he paid me a visit. He stood in the corner of the room wearing briefs and an olive-drab T-shirt.

". . . and I just want to grab that fucker by the scruff of his neck" (he was talking about a celebrated wide receiver for the Dallas Cowboys who'd recently had a number of setbacks related to an incorrigible cocaine habit), "and say 'Listen, you stupid nigger: Stop acting like a fucking *six*-year-old and get off your pathetic lazy ass and get your shit together' . . ."

This from a guy who'd taken more than his share of drugs and only minutes before had laughed at the idea of ever getting a job. In the past I would have assayed some witticism or pointed remark—"I can think of any *number* of people who'd benefit from such advice"—but this time I hesitated, too bemused or perhaps intimidated to speak. I wondered if my brother picked up on the irony and was daring me to be a smartass about it. But I don't think so. I don't think any irony occurred to him. Anyway, he broadened his attack to include black people in general.

"Face it, Zwieb, niggers are despicable. It's all about who's the biggest *pimp* and who's fucked the most *bitches* and, you know, *killed* the most people."

I was sorry to hear Scott say this. One of his most endearing traits had always been a steadfast sympathy for black people and anyone else who was treated unfairly by the world. His hero (with John Lennon) had been Muhammad Ali at a time when I myself thought the man was a cocky bastard who needed to get his head knocked off. Granted I was a child, but Scott was only a little older and his friends felt the same way I did.

I said that it was more a question of class than race. I pointed out that my own black students were mostly middle-class and pretty much indistinguishable from their white counterparts, which wasn't strictly true but I thought it best not to get bogged down in nuance.

"I mean racism is pretty cretinous, Scott. I hope it's just a passing phase."

He stood swaying a bit in his underwear, thinking it over, and I glanced wistfully at my book. Finally he gulped the dregs of his beer and daintily smacked his lips as though he were drinking it just for the taste, then squeezed my shoulder a bit too hard and left the room.

THE NEXT MORNING he was full of beans. I'd slept on the couch in the living room—the spare bedroom was taken by Scott and his things—and I awoke to the huff and thump of jumping jacks. It was very cold outside, and Scott wore a stocking cap but no shirt. He was in good shape, remarkably so for a drunk, but then he'd always had better muscle tone than I.

"Sorry, Zwieb," he said, "but I couldn't wait any longer. Gotta get some PT in."

"By all means."

He counted fifty, flourished a hand, and trotted out the door. I smelled coffee and found my mother in the kitchen feeding her cats—or rather opening cans and mixing wet food with dry, though no cats appeared. In the past they'd always swarmed purring around her legs, all seven or eight of them (with more outside), rushing into the kitchen at the first click of the can opener.

"Where are they?" I asked. "Where's Sam and Sophie and—"

I realized I hadn't seen a single cat since I'd arrived. But here was my mother feeding them.

She shook her head. "They're hiding. They won't come out until Scott's been gone a while. I think he *did* something to them." She gave a gusty sigh.

"Poor sweetie."

"At first I had to make excuses to get him out of the house so they'd eat. 'Scott, have you weeded the garden yet?' Something like that. But then he got so goddamn *lazy* I couldn't ask him to do anything, so I just said 'Scott, get outta here! The cats need to eat!' " Marlies's cats were the love of her life. Her frown trembled with a tough look; she was trying not to cry. "And he said 'Let 'em eat, then.' And I said 'Don't gimme that, buster. You know they won't eat around you.' And he gives me this innocent look: 'Why not?' 'Because,' I said"—she leveled a spatula at my face as if I were Scott—" 'they *hate* you!'" She nodded with satisfaction. "Son of a bitch."

After the cats were fed, or rather the food was laid out, my mother cooked breakfast and we took our plates into the living room. On the table I noticed the Modern Library edition of *A Fan's Notes* that I'd sent Scott for his birthday the year before last. I'd inscribed the flyleaf as follows: "There's a little Exley in all of us (though more in some than others). Happy 37th! Love, Z." I asked my mother if she wanted me to read to her, and she nodded at the ceiling. She was lying on the couch with a plate propped on her belly. A cat appeared out of nowhere and began lapping up her egg yolk; my mother did nothing to stop him. She stroked the cat gratefully and shut her eyes. The cat moved on to her sausage. Other cats had begun swishing furtively into the kitchen. I was reading to my mother when suddenly the cats scattered and the screen door whacked shut: Scott. He stood at the head of the couch and placed a cold hand on my mother's cheek. She looked too tired to recoil. He gestured for me to keep reading and listened with a little smile, tracing a finger over his muscular chest. I read another page or so from the first chapter, all about the events leading up to the narrator's latest alcoholic collapse. My brother laughed wheezily. Exley had just taken an oblivious piss in the middle of the street when my mother announced: "Stop. I don't like this man." She took our plates to the kitchen and began washing up.

"That's great, Zwieb," Scott remarked. "I mean it's not only entertaining but the guy has a real ear for language. Every sentence is kind of"—he paused for the right word—"lapidary."

I nodded. "But you've already read it, right? At least this chapter?"

He shook his head with a little moonbeam smile.

"But I don't get it, Scott. This is practically the story of your life! And if you agree it's entertaining and well-written—'lapidary,' no less—then why the hell don't you read it?" I laughed. "I mean why not? Seriously."

But he only shrugged, smiling, and left to take a shower. The point was this: he knew a well-turned phrase when he heard it, his critical-aesthetic faculties were intact more or less, but his book-reading days were over. It would no more occur to him to read a book—literature anyway: a nonutile work of fiction—than it would to get a job, and that was simply that.

MY MOTHER AND I spent the second day of my visit running errands. Over breakfast Scott had babbled on about his lawsuit (he expected that damages would run in the millions), and now he asked to come along, but my mother put her foot down.

"I want to spend time with your *brother*," she snapped. "*Alone.*"

Scott narrowed his eyes at the TV and forced a little smirk. When sober he picked his battles, and for her part my mother became her old bullying self, venting the bitterness she'd bottled up while he was drunk and abusive. This, in turn, made Scott all the more abusive once he was drunk again. It was easy to see where things were heading.

"So when's he moving out?" I asked in the car.

My mother, who'd just started to relax a little, got an almost frantic look. *"I don't want to talk about it! I don't want to talk about it! It's Christmas! Can't we just be pleasant for an hour or so!"*

I found a radio station playing Muzak carols and we stopped talking.

I often think my mother is happiest when she's grocery shopping, and the half hour or so we spent trawling the aisles at Albertson's was pretty much the high point of our holiday. My mother likes to kvetch at the butchers, whom she knows by name: "Paul! Where're those lamb kidneys you were going to save me!" Or: "You call that a hock? I want a *big* one!" And Paul (or whoever) would smile in a silly-me sort of way and fetch what she'd asked for. I imagine if I ever addressed a butcher like that he'd sink a cleaver in my head, but it was okay in her case. She was the eccentric German lady, a little spot of color in their workaday lives.

"What shall we have?" she asked me, rhetorically, rubbing her palms as she surveyed the meat bins. "A lovely duck?"

"Sure," I said.

"Pick one."

I picked a duck. My mother batted it out of my hands.

"*No-oo!* You call that a duck?" She grabbed a proper duck and dragged the cart along. Whenever we shopped I'd make a show of pushing the cart while my mother bustled in front yanking it this way and that; if I let go, she'd snap, "Push the cart! Do I have to do *everything*?"

"What about herring?" she asked. "You want some herring?"

"Herring?"

She put a jar of pickled herring in the cart. "For herring salad, dummy."

"Right."

I was happy to play the dummy, the doormat, happy to see my mother enjoying herself.

Next we went to Barnes & Noble to finish our Christmas shopping; it was cold enough to leave the groceries out in the car. I bought Scott a couple of videos: some sort of rockumentary and *Annie Hall*, the high points of which he'd once recited at the dinner table twenty years before (while implying how stoned he'd been during the movie, the better for us to admire his talent for retention). As a stocking stuffer I also picked up a little one-dollar Penguin minipaperback of Chekhov's long story "The Black Monk." Scott wouldn't read it, of course, but I looked forward to letting him know it was about a young lunatic whose only reasons for living are his delusions of grandeur: "His 'black monk' is a bit like your 'lawsuit,' " I'd explain, since I still thought the key to my brother's better self was his sense of humor.

It was late afternoon by the time we got back, and I was surprised to find Scott only a little sodden. His face was oily with the few beers he'd drunk, but he still smelled of soap and his eyes were clear. I was about to commend him for his restraint when he waved me into his room.

"Zwieb," he said in a stage whisper. "There's no liquor in the house."

"Well," I said, "but that's part of the deal. You're not supposed to have liquor, right?"

My poor mother, I thought. In order to reform a lunatic she'd sacrificed one of the great comforts of her life (and mine), the nightly cocktails. Another comfort was her cats. That left gardening, grocery shopping, and cooking.

"It's her house," I added.

He socked me playfully in the arm. "C'mon, Zwieb! It's Christmas! Don't you want a cocktail?"

What it amounted to was this: he was driving to the liquor store one way or the other, and it would look better if he did so at least partly on my behalf. Two against one. I told him he was captain of his soul, a middle-aged man with a car, and if he wanted to go to the liquor store I couldn't stop him. As for our mother, what could she do?

"Fuck right!"

He wasn't whispering anymore, provoked by my "middle-aged man with a car" crack. A minute later he whacked out the door, tripping a bit on the ice when my mother called, *"Scott, where are you going?"* He didn't answer.

"He's off to the liquor store," I said, and she sagged against the wall. Such was her despair that she didn't bother to berate me for failing to talk him out of it.

AS IT HAPPENED Marlies had some brandy stashed away, and as soon as Scott's car had sizzled into the distance she asked me to retrieve the bottle. She stayed put in the kitchen. Once the drinks were poured she staggered to the breakfast bar and we stood slumped on either side, talking and drinking. I told her the situation was bad, worse than I'd expected, and she agreed with a heavy nod. She wanted to be rid of him but didn't quite know how to go about it. She admitted she was a little frightened of him, which meant she was terrified. He seemed capable of anything. She told me other things he'd said and done in the two months he'd been there, none so bad as kneeing her in the groin (she showed me part of a hideous bruise on her inner thigh) but ominous in terms of their escalating audacity.

After a while we noticed the time and agreed Scott had been delayed. It didn't take more than forty-five minutes or so to drive to the liquor store and back, even in this weather.

"Maybe he's dead or injured," I said wistfully.

"Unkraut vergeht nicht," my mother sighed, as ever, whereupon the phone rang. We knew it was Scott. I think we even knew why. This had been going on for almost a quarter of a century, after all.

Sure enough he'd wrecked his car.

"How bad is it?" my mother asked, and by the way she winced I knew Scott's reply had been abusive. It was bad; the poor old car was history. The word "fuck" squawked out of the receiver at intervals. My mother went on questioning him with a sort of meek Socratic irony.

"Whose fault is it? ... Are you okay? ... Are the police there? ... Are you drunk?"

Alas, he was sober more or less, and the liquor he'd bought at the store was still unopened, which meant he wouldn't be arrested on the spot. In fact he'd only gotten a ticket for reckless driving, and what's more the obliging policemen were going to bring him back to us safe and sound.

ALL TOO SHORTLY thereafter, Scott banged through the door lugging a large plastic storage bin he'd kept in the trunk of his BMW—an essential item from the days when he'd lived out of his car. But his car was no more. What was left was the bin, which clanked and tinkled as he laid it heavily on the kitchen floor. It was full of clothes and the bottles he'd bought at the liquor store. Brazenly he uncapped a liter of Jim Beam and took a lavish swig. *"Ahhh!"* he said, and belched.

"Scott, you can't drink that in here!"

My mother.

"Yeah, Scott," I said, "drink it *outside*."

Nobody laughed. With one bloodshot eye on both of us, he took another swig and belched again. I thought of the time twenty years ago when my father had brought him back, bandanna and all, from the police station. Here was the same swollen face, the same pathetic swagger, the same defiant self-pity vis-à-vis a world that refused to cut him a break.

My mother took a different tack. With a sort of censure-free eagerness, she asked my brother to explain, in detail, what had happened exactly, as though he were a famous raconteur and we were his audience, all agog.

"What the fuck difference does it make?" he said, but with a little coaxing he admitted that the motorist in front of him had seen fit to stop at a yellow light, while he, Scott, had kept going. The fucking *ice* and so forth.

"Is he all right?" my mother asked.

Scott closed his eyes, stock-still with exquisite patience. "Who?"

"The man in the other car!"

Scott said the *woman* was fine, though he would have preferred to "maim the cunt." He laughed at his own ugliness. Not for the first time he seemed intrigued by the duality of his own nature—that he could be a good Christian (as he still considered himself) on the one hand and say things like "maim the cunt" on the other. He added that he'd like to get all such cunts off the roads. For good.

"That would leave the roads to yourself," I observed, "and people like yourself."

Marlies, perhaps to distract him, pointed out that the woman had probably sustained some degree of whiplash and would almost certainly sue. She noted as much with a kind of ponderous objectivity. It was a very German thing to say: actions have consequences; if you suck your thumb the tailor will cut it off, etc. Scott let it be known that he didn't give a fuck what either woman—my mother or the motorist—said or did.

Then they resumed wrangling over whether Scott had any right to drink liquor in my mother's house. Scott's position was that life was one fucking thing after another, and now he'd lost his car, a car that had served him faithfully for six years, and by God in light of all that he was going to get drunk tonight and nobody was going to stop him.

Made sense to me. "Look," I said. "I'm going to the other room and watch TV. Scott, I don't give a fuck if you drink yourself to *death*, but could you do it in your own room and quietly, please? And Ma. Give it a rest already. I mean really, who the fuck cares?"

Neither replied. They were waiting for me to leave. They still had a lot to say to each other, and I had no part in that conversation. I was an outsider; I didn't grasp the principles at stake, and they weren't going to explain them to me.

LATER I LAY awake in the dark, an iron poker within reach under the couch. A faint light from my brother's room was visible in the hall. Every half hour or so the following would occur: my mother would pad lightly through the living room, so not to wake me, and turn down the thermostat in the hall; my brother, drunk, kept turning it up to eighty or so. Then she'd open my brother's door—quietly—and hiss at him to leave the thermostat alone and go to *sleep* already. Scott would remonstrate after a fashion. This would go on for maybe five minutes; then my mother would return to her room. Moments later Scott would turn up the thermostat again, the vents would roar, and my mother would pad lightly through the living room again.

At one point I distinctly heard my brother say, "You touch that thermostat again I'm gonna fuckin *kill* you."

The tension must have overwhelmed me, because I fell asleep after that. My mother woke me in the morning. She was kneeling beside the couch.

"Now that his car's gone he'll never leave!" she said in a gaspy hysterical whisper. "You have to tell him to go! You have to get him out of here!"

I was struck by the contrast between her mad tenacity the night before—her refusal to relinquish the thermostat prerogative—and her utter helplessness now. She was done in. She was like the proverbial frog in the skillet that doesn't jump because the heat is turned up slowly, slowly, until the frog dies.

"So what finally happened with the thermostat?" I asked.

She shot an anxious glance over her shoulder. Beckoned me into the hall. Scott's door was slightly ajar. She pushed it aside—a chilly whiff of bourbon and body odor ensued—and there was Scott, naked, in a shivering fetal lump beside a floor vent. My mother had outlasted him *re* the thermostat, a Pyrrhic victory to be sure: he'd passed out before he could kill her. She closed the door and tugged me into the kitchen.

"What am I gonna *do*?" she asked.

I'd given this a lot of thought the night before, while I lay in the dark listening to the same argument (more or less: the thermostat was just the latest MacGuffin) they'd been having since Scott was thirteen or so. I reminded my mother that she was supposed to take me into town that day so I could rent a car and drive to Oklahoma City and see some friends; instead we'd go to the police station and arrange for Scott's removal from the premises.

My mother looked doubtful. "You mean have him arrested?"

"Well, if that's what it takes, sure."

"No, sweetie." She shook her head. "I can't do that. It's Christmas."

"He threatened to kill you last night! He *will* kill you." Her head was still wagging faintly, so I slung my bolt. "Think of your cats."

About an hour later I heard Scott stirring and caught a glimpse of him as he slipped out the door and hurried into the bathroom. His face was set with a kind of petulant dignity; he was no longer naked. Rather he wore one of the ankle-length Wee Willie Winkie nightshirts he'd affected ever since his teen years—the bedtime equivalent of his trench coats and caps. He took a long shower, rushed back to his room with eyes averted (petulantly), and finally emerged wearing a respectable sweater and slacks. He took his place behind my mother in the kitchen and waited to be noticed; my mother went on chopping onions. At last he spoke with a fussy little clearing of his throat:

"I apologize for whatever *inconvenience* my behavior might have caused you last night. I suppose I was feeling, you know, *distressed*, given the fact that I'd lost the one possession that matters to me in the whole world, but I guess that's no reason to, ah, to *inflict* my bad fortune on others. So I hope we can put this behind us and enjoy our Christmas."

The speech—nine parts self-pity and one part sarcastic contrition—was not apt to move even the softest heart to forgiveness, and my mother was not moved. I did notice, however, a slight flicker of guilt around her mouth, but she visibly toughened as she considered her cats.

"What d'you want for breakfast?" she said in a neutral voice. Scott answered and seemed about to resume the speech, but my mother sighed in a let's-just-forget-it sort of way, and Scott seemed glad enough to leave her. I received him in the manner of a bantering little bro' in some suburban sitcom.

"Hey, Slick! How's the morning head?"

Scott seemed relieved, if a bit warily so, and made some bantering reply. Somewhere in the midst of our bantering I noticed the poker peeking out from under the couch and pushed it out of sight with my foot.

Somehow we got through breakfast and finally, with the exhilaration of tunneling convicts, my mother and I made it out to the car. Scott was framed pensively in the doorway, watching us. As ever he'd wanted to come along.

"Don't forget," I said, as my mother drove carefully over the ice, "to mention the fact that he assaulted you."

But she wouldn't hear of it. She wanted to *help* Scott, she said; maybe the police could persuade him to get treatment. In any event she had no intention of saying anything that might get him arrested. She just wanted him out of her house, period. She went on like this all the way to the police station.

We had to wait in the lobby for a few minutes, and I used the time to cancel my lunch appointment with an old friend.

"Sorry, Chris," I said, when his machine beeped, "but my brother Scott threatened to kill my mother last night so now we're at the police station and it looks like it might take a while. Rain check? Well . . . wish me luck!"

Then we were sitting in a cubicle opposite a police officer, who asked Marlies a series of deadpan questions and jotted some notes.

"And you say he's violent?"

"Well—he's *potentially* violent. He drinks!"

The cop made note of this. "So he hasn't actually done anything to you?"

"Can't we just take him to the hospital?" my mother pleaded. "I want to *help* him. He needs *help*."

"He's violent," I told the policeman. "He assaulted her and he's capable of worse. A lot worse. Last night he threatened to kill her."

"He did not!"

"He did too."

"He was drunk!"

"Right. He drunkenly threatened to kill her, and he's drunk

most of the time. It's like saying he was breathing at the time."
The cop mirthlessly jotted this down, and I mentioned a few other
salient details. "He needs to be institutionalized," I said. "A mental hospital would be nice, I guess, but we'll settle for prison."

"We will *not*!" said my mother.

The man put down his pencil. Arching his eyebrows as he
scanned his notes, he advised us that the best they could do was
remove Scott as a trespasser. They'd be happy to do this.

"Can't you take him to a hospital?" my mother asked.

"With his consent, sure."

I laughed. "What about some kind of restraining order?"

The cop replied that some kind of order—not exactly a "restraining order" per se, but some lesser equivalent—could be issued
under the following conditions: if, having been removed as a trespasser, Scott were to come within a hundred feet of us and still be
imminent and menacing by the time the police arrived, we could
petition the court for an order; then, if he returned *again* after that,
and was *again* willing to wait around for the police without maim-
ing or killing us, he could at last be arrested.

"Sounds dicey," I said.

The cop frowned in a noncommittal way. "So. Would you like
him removed from your property?"

"Yes, please."

WE RENDEZVOUSED WITH a police car about a mile from
my mother's house. One of the cops was a burly guy in his fifties
with a walrus mustache that seemed to capture the gravity of the
situation. He explained what was about to go down. He assured
my anxious mother that Scott wouldn't be arrested or molested
in any way as long as he didn't resist. He advised us to stay in the

background and let them handle it. His partner, a tense younger man, gave a sharp affirmative nod: *just so.*

Scott didn't answer the door right away. I worried that he'd spotted the police car and bolted out a back window—waiting in the woods until the coast was clear to kill us—but then the door swung open and there was Scott. For a moment he registered faint surprise: his eyes narrowed and he cocked his head slightly; then, darting a glance at me, our mother, and back at the cops, he said:

"Won't you come in, officers?"

When sober Scott understood that it didn't pay to mince words with cops; this was one nugget of wisdom he'd culled from his dark sojourn. His voice was soft, concerned—*what could the trouble be?*—and when the tense cop asked him to step away from the door, Scott obliged with hasty composure. Then, with an almost comic diffidence—a mildly flustered butler—he invited the cops to follow him into the living room and have a seat. They remained standing. Scott asked if they minded whether *he* sat; they did not. Scott arranged himself in a chair, crossing his legs, and waited for the matter to be explained to him.

"Sir," said the walrus mustache, "your mother would like you to leave her house."

Scott gave our mother a wondering look: *surely not.*

"Scott, you need help," she said. "You're an alcoholic and you need help."

"An 'alcoholic'?" He slowly shook his head, as though he didn't quite get the joke. "Because I got a little drunk last night, I'm suddenly an 'alcoholic' . . . ?"

I thought about interjecting a scornful laugh at that point, but decided to stand on my dignity. I sighed and gave the officers a vaguely pained look.

"Scott," said my mother, "please let these men take you to the VA."

"I'm not going to a hospital. There's nothing wrong with me." He considered the matter further and added, "It's Christmas!" And there was real dudgeon in his voice. Christmas was sacred to Scott: it meant family and good food and booze and carols and Christ and an overall serenity that was otherwise missing from his life.

"Christmas is canceled this year," said my mother.

"Well," said Scott, "Christmas is *on* as far as I'm concerned."

I sighed again, a definitive sigh, a sigh that called for an end to the whole charade. With reticent dignity I approached the older cop and asked where Scott would be taken if not to a hospital. The man replied at length. He said that Scott would be taken to the end of the long gravel driveway leading to the main road, where he'd have to wait for a cab. And yes, the cops would keep Scott company and make sure he got into the cab. In a kindly reminiscent way, the man went on about various contingencies that sometimes arose in this sort of dispute. He took no account of Scott's presence as he spoke, though I could feel Scott's stare on the back of my neck. At one point I turned slightly and Scott managed to lock eyes with me (the cop was still talking) in a way that was, I think, meant to intimidate and yet also appeal to my finer feelings. His eyes were brimming with hatred, with love, with sadness that it had come, at last, to this.

"I bet you're enjoying yourself," he said.

"It's one of the worst experiences of my life," I replied.

This sounded maudlin and a little craven, but I was mostly in earnest. It was a bad time, all right. But then, too, such a remark was precisely the sort of thing you say if you're posing as the Good Son, the mature one who only wants what's best for his long-suffering mother and so on. Which is to say, I *was* enjoying myself rather.

"Well, it's almost over," said Scott. "For now."

"You hear that?" I asked the older cop, who closed his eyes and nodded. He was a decent man who found such matters regrettable.

The cops took over from there. The younger one followed Scott to his room and stood in the doorway while he packed his things. Now and then the man chuckled a little nervously, and I knew Scott was trying to charm him, to win him over with jokey bravado: "Well, *this* is a hell of a note! Frankly, I hope those two get *coal* in their stockings . . ." Drawers opened and shut with judicious restraint, wire hangers tinkled lightly. Finally Scott emerged with his duffel bag flung over his back; he looked as though he'd decided to find the whole thing amusing, though I could tell he wasn't amused. He dropped his bag in the living room and turned to the cops.

"I want you guys to know," he said, "that I find your professionalism commendable. You couldn't have been more courteous and kind, and I want you to know I'll never forget it."

On the simplest level, Scott was being sincere—the policemen *were* nice blokes. On another level, he meant to contrast their niceness with his family's vicious duplicity (at Christmas no less), suggesting that someday, perhaps, he'd be in a position to repay both kindness and cruelty. On a final, murkier level, he was casting ahead to some future court hearing: *No, the defendant was perfectly polite. He seemed genuinely perplexed and saddened by the whole* . . .

"Scott—your presents—" said Marlies, gathering them out from under the tree. When Scott seemed hesitant to accept them, she dropped to her knees and began packing them expertly in his duffel bag. Two things occurred to me: one, that only my mother would dare take such a liberty, and two, that Scott was traveling light under the circumstances (he hadn't packed the rest of his liquor—this for the sake of appearances, no doubt, though I found it ominous).

Finally he stood at the kitchen bar consulting the Yellow Pages for a motel. "That place is good," the younger cop suggested, tapping his finger on a particular listing. "Clean and cheap and kinda in-between here and the city." Scott nodded and phoned for a reservation; then he called a cab and gave the dispatcher patient directions to our remote location. Hanging up, he stood there shaking his head, as if the whole business were simply too bizarre for words.

"Ma, you're not really serious about this," he said. "C'mon. I'm your *son*, for crying out loud. It's Christmas."

"You brought this on yourself!" said my mother, with her stolid Germanic fondness for platitudes.

"Oh yeah, and life's been so *good* to me," he said.

I could restrain myself no longer. Sneeringly I pointed out—not for the first time—that it was always *life's* fault as opposed to Scott's own.

He took a step in my direction. The older cop saw me brace myself and grabbed Scott by the arm. The younger cop, a little hesitantly, took the other arm, and Scott went comically limp in their grasp. As they led him toward the door, he leaned back and bugged his eyes at me: *"See you soo-oon!"* he called, with loony menace, and then he was gone.

THE FIRST ORDER of business was buying a gun. My mother had nothing but an old varmint rifle that looked as if it hadn't been fired since the Alamo, and besides there were no bullets.

After checking the Yellow Pages (still open to the motel list-
ings), we drove to a sporting goods emporium on the interstate,
where I explained our needs to a bearded fellow in the gun
department. He wore a camouflage jacket and squinted intently
with one eye.

"What you need it for?" he asked, when I mentioned that I
hadn't fired a gun since childhood and didn't want anything fancy.

"Self-defense," I said. "To shoot, you know—people."

"*Nuh!*" my mother protested.

The man nodded and ducked under the counter, coming up
with a snub-nose pistol in a chamois cloth. "This here's what you
want," he said. "Smith and Wesson .38, just point and fire."

I paid with American Express and presented the neat plastic
gun case to my mother. Merry Christmas. Then we went to a Chi-
nese restaurant and discussed strategy over martinis and spare
ribs.

"Okay, so you're holding the gun," I said. "What do you say?"

" 'Sit down.' "

"And if he doesn't? What if he comes toward you?"

"I *shoot* him," she said, and took a giggly sip of gin.

We were both feeling the strain, but I enjoined her to be serious. I'd warned her and warned her and *warned* her about Scott,
and now look what had happened! With tipsy solemnity I added
that if she ever let Scott into her life again, *ever*, I'd wash my hands
of them both.

She nodded a trifle absently. "Fine."

"Fine what?"

She shrugged. "Scott's not as bad as you think. It's not all black
and white, you know. There's a little gray!"

"*There's a little gray.* Gosh, I hadn't thought of that! Got a pen?
I want to write that down . . ." Thus my father used to mock her

platitudes. She smiled reminiscently. "Look," I said. "From now on—and I think your cats would agree with me—it's all black. No gray. If you want to indulge grayness, you do it on your own. Understood?"

She nodded.

"Okay. So you've got the gun. What do you say?"

" 'Sit down.' "

"And if he doesn't?"

She thumped the table with a meaty fist. "I *shoot* the bastard."

IT WAS GETTING dark by the time we stopped at Walmart to buy bullets. A spindly blue-vested adolescent yanked out a tray of cartridges and said that these here (pointing) were the hollow-tipped kind and that's what we wanted. "Goes in like that," he said, making a little half-inch hole with thumb and forefinger, "and comes out like *this*," whereupon he described a bloated grapefruit with both hands. We bought a box of twenty-five. "So much for just winging him," I remarked.

I should add that earlier, as we were leaving the restaurant, I'd called Scott's motel to see whether he'd checked in. He hadn't, or else he'd done so under an assumed name. Probably, though, he was lurking around the house somewhere, waiting for us to return, and if our luck had *really* gone south he'd managed to find a gun of his own. One remembered his time as a marksmanship instructor in the marines. My mother pulled off the gravel driveway, and we took turns firing into a pond embankment. Fat gobs of mud spattered on impact; a dark curtain of birds flushed into the air. Somewhere, perhaps, Scott was listening.

The house was a vague silhouette in the powdery twilight. When my mother stopped the car I rolled out the passenger side, literally rolled, in the manner of some intrepid TV cop; half-consciously I thought if Scott were watching from his hiding place, he wouldn't be able to restrain his laughter and then I'd have the drop on him. Cocking the gun at my ear, I scampered like a troll from bush to bush, casing the house—peeking in windows, pausing in a crouch to fan the gun at the darkling woods, and so on. Finally I made the entire circuit and gave my mother a thumbs-up. She hopped out of her car and trotted with awkward haste up the icy path, fumbling in her purse for the house keys. An oddly poignant sight.

It took a while for the adrenaline to wear off. We turned on every light in the house and closed the curtains, triple-locked the doors; then my mother poured herself some brandy and made phone calls: to a Realtor friend who could get her a deal on a fancy alarm system—indeed could arrange for installation first thing in the morning if not that very night—and to various others who knew Scott and promised to let us know if they gained some inkling of his whereabouts. After the last phone call, my mother drank off her brandy and joined me on the couch, where I sat watching TV with the gun in my lap. A few minutes later the phone rang. We stayed put.

"I think it's pretty poor," Scott's voice slurred over the machine, "pretty fucking *piss* poor that I have to spend Christmas in some fleabag motel. I'm thirty-eight years old," he added, and lapsed into a long drunken silence. My mother started to get up, and I pulled her back down on the couch. "*Stille Nacht, heilige Nacht,*" Scott began to sing, "*alles schläft, einsam wacht . . .*" At last he sighed, took a drink (ice tinkling), and hung up.

So he was, it seemed, at some motel—doubtless a real fleabag rather than the "clean" place suggested by the cop, since Scott didn't mind a certain kind of tidy squalor and of course he'd want to husband his money for liquor and drugs. That was reassuring. My mother and I laughed a little, and even waited somewhat hopefully for Scott to call again and perhaps sing another carol.

The rest of the evening was pleasant enough. We sat around drinking Scott's liquor and opening a few early Christmas presents. My mother had some kind of Hopi prayer stick or incense wand, and at one point she lighted this and walked all around the house—a wobbly but dignified saunter—waving smoke at whatever remained of Scott's spirit. One by one her cats came out of hiding and joined us there in the living room as though nothing had ever been amiss.

Scott called again around 3:00 A.M., and roughly four times a day after that. Drunk or sober he was unrepentant, but not really vengeful: as usual he tried alternately to sweet-talk our mother and make her feel guilty, but she only kept repeating that mantra about his bringing it all on himself, which must have driven him up the wall. I worried she'd relent as soon as I returned to New Orleans, but happily Scott was arrested on a public-drunk charge and back in jail by the new year.

part V

the calm mid-heaven

One good thing about that last harrowing Christmas with Scott was that it led, for a time, to reconciliation between my father and me. We hadn't spoken in almost two years when I called him that day at his office to let him know I'd just bought a gun—this shortly after I'd learned that Scott hadn't checked in at the "clean" motel. I asked my father if maybe he'd be willing to hire a private detective to find Scott and follow him around, or better yet arrange via his friend the DA for Scott to be arrested on some trumped-up charge. Though Burck kept his own counsel with regard to these rather wayward suggestions, he was calm and kind and comforting to talk to. He asked me to keep him posted, which I did, and we met for lunch a few days later.

Talking about Scott became more and more painful for my father, and it was understood one didn't broach the subject without his implicit consent. Sandra, however, *liked* to talk about Scott, as he remained a danger as long as he was alive and it made sense to inquire about his whereabouts; also he was just a fascinating subject. My father was still at his office in the city when Mary and I arrived at Breeze Hill for a visit—our first—so we sat in the kitchen with Sandra and Kelli (whom I hadn't seen in six years, since that awful ski trip to Santa Fe), chatting, easily enough, about Scott.

"Listen, you guys," Sandra said, lowering her voice and edging closer in her chair, "I've never told this to a soul—well, I've never told your *father* . . ."

Kelli nodded. She knew what was coming.

"But one time, Scott *kissed* me."

Mary glanced at me with furtive puzzlement: *What's wrong with that?* I remained poker-faced.

"You mean he kissed you on the cheek?" I said. "Or what?"

Sandra slowly shook her head. She pulled her chair a bit closer. "He kissed me on the *lips*," she all but whispered. "He kissed me with his *tongue*."

Kelli chuckled in a worldly sort of way. She'd lived in San Francisco for some ten years by then and was little fazed by the endless oddity of human conduct.

"It was right after we moved here," Sandra said. "I think it was the first time Scott spent the night . . ."

Her voice became a little rushed and flustered as it occurred to her that my brother had been welcome at the ranch right up to the time he went to prison almost, a time when I myself—a schoolteacher of decent repute—would have been escorted off the grounds by hired hands, Jack barking viciously in my wake.

"...and your father had left for the day, or maybe he was out with the horses? I don't know. Anyway he wasn't around. So we were here in the kitchen, Scott and me, and I think maybe I'd packed him a lunch for the road—maybe that was it: I'd packed him lunch! Anyway he wanted to thank me for the lunch. I don't know. Anyway you guys: he took my face in his hands and he *kissed* me."

She stared at the memory, freshly aghast.

Poor Scott. Briefly, briefly, as a boy on the verge of manhood, he'd been so handsome and promising that the sequel must have seemed a dream; behind the acne and brain damage and bewildering alienation, he was a golden boy still. Probably he thought he'd given his poor old stepmom the thrill of her life. One thing was certain: at that moment he'd loved her and was sorry for ever thinking ill of her—she'd packed his lunch!—and wanted to convey this in some meaningful way. Probably, too, he was drunk and/or high.

As Scott's only brother—a person who shared his sense of humor and some of his darker tendencies too—I considered explaining as much to Sandra, for what it was worth. Instead I said, "Welcome to the club."

"...No!"

I nodded. "Tongue and all."

Sandra and Mary were speechless, but Kelli only wagged her head and looked more worldly than ever.

"Scott's not going to make it in this life," she sighed. But she was smiling too. The implication was that perhaps he'd fare better in the *next* life. At the time, oddly enough, it was a comforting and not implausible thought.

I LISTENED GRUDGINGLY whenever my mother shared news of Scott. Her obsession with the subject was exasperating.

She missed Scott and wanted to talk about him, simple as that—to speculate about his motives, to retrace our steps to the exact point when everything went blooey.

At the time his life was either picaresque or tragic, depending on how you look at it. After that last Christmas en famille, Scott got out of jail with the help of an old gay friend of my mother, Roger, the man who used to tell me about his 160 IQ. Roger was now a lonely sexagenarian living in Hawaii (where he and Scott had renewed their acquaintance while Scott was in the marines). As a purely philanthropic gesture—so my mother was given to understand—Roger flew my brother to the islands and gave him a place to stay.

"Isn't that great?" said my mother. "He's thousands of miles away! And he *loves* Hawaii! Maybe he'll . . ."

I guess it was maybe three weeks later that Scott beat the shit out of poor old Roger, who'd made the mistake of insisting that Scott not drink another beer, since they'd agreed to hold the line at a six-pack a day or something. But one night Scott took a seventh or eighth or twentieth out of the fridge; Roger picked up the phone and threatened to call the cops, whereupon Scott wrested the phone away and used it to cudgel his benefactor senseless.

Scott was homeless after that, but the Hawaiian climate was gentle and for a while he did all right. He slept in parks and churches, ate at shelters, and used his VA pension for liquor and drugs. I suspect he stole quite a lot too, and then Marlies would send him a little something from time to time, whenever Scott would call her to announce he was ready to turn over a new leaf.

"He's taking classes," she told me one night. "Isn't that great? He's enrolled at the University of Hawaii!"

Toward the end of her life, Oma from Vinita was cheerfully senile, and would go on and on about all the wonderful things she'd done in her ninety-plus years. For example, she was under the impression that she'd ridden with Bob Hope (or Elizabeth Taylor or Marlon Brando) in a hot-air balloon over the Atlantic. Why not? "Wow," I'd say, patting her desiccated hand, "you've had an incredible life, Oma." But I rather doubt that Oma, even there at the end, would have believed that Scott was enrolled at the University of Hawaii.

"Scott's not enrolled at the University of Hawaii," I said. "Scott will *never* be enrolled at the University of Hawaii."

Pause. "How do you know?" my mother asked, with genuine curiosity, as if I were privy to some special intelligence.

I didn't know what to say. I'd said it all a thousand, thousand times. One tried to be kind. "Mom, just call the registrar's office. They'll tell you. Or don't. It doesn't really matter, I guess."

"But how do you *know* . . . ?"

For the next few weeks I considered calling the University of Hawaii myself and putting the matter triumphantly to rest, but then I forgot about it, and finally Scott spared us any further curiosity by getting arrested and going back to prison. He assured my mother it was a travesty of justice and asked her to contact the ACLU on his behalf.

A YEAR AFTER Scott's arrest, I was married in Scotland— the Isle of Mull, to be exact, populated almost entirely by sheep, whose company we preferred for that sort of thing. Mary looked lovely as we took our vows; there were rose petals on the coverlet back at our seventeenth-century inn amid the heathery hills of Dervaig. After a week of blessed isolation, we met my father and Sandra in London, where as luck would have it an International Bar Association conference was in progress. There were a few awkward moments—Sandra felt strongly that my wife should *not* have kept her name—but the worst seemed behind us.

So we went home and pleasantly took up our lives. I resumed trying to write, and my wife entered a prestigious doctoral program. We began to talk about kids. When, rarely, a cloud scudded into my purview, I had only to remind myself that Scott was in prison and the sun would shine again, more or less.

THEN SUDDENLY (though in fact three years had passed) he wasn't. During an otherwise happy Christmas, my mother was contacted by a shyster Scott had hired. The man could get Scott out of prison, he explained, if we could arrange for him to leave Hawaii. Scott, of course, was eager to come home again.

"Well, that's easy," I told my mother. "Just don't pay for his plane ticket."

"But it's his money!" she said. "How do you think he hired the lawyer?"

As it happened Scott's financial affairs were in good order, thanks to Marlies, who'd arranged for his monthly VA checks to be deposited into a high-interest savings account. Quite a bundle had piled up over the years, and what could my mother do now but fork it over? We quarreled hideously about it, and I invoked my old threat to wash my hands of them both. My mother's position, as ever, was that *somebody* had to help Scott or he'd lose hope altogether. My position was that losing hope was *good* in Scott's case; losing hope was *sensible*. But Marlies saw herself as the last buffer between a hopeless, desperate, possibly homicidal Scott and the rest of us—me, Mary, Burck, even Sandra. At length she confided that, indeed, Scott had often indulged in reveries of harming us: we'd betrayed and abandoned him, after all, and besides we were nonbelievers—his was the Sword of Righteousness and so forth.

"Why don't you notify the fucking authorities?" I asked her. "Call the warden in Hawaii and *say* he's making these threats, for Christ's sake! We don't need *you* as a buffer! We need iron bars! We need the Pacific Ocean!"

But we needn't have worried. The Scott who left prison in January 2003 was pretty much incapable of harming anyone but himself, and this he did promptly. The day after his release he fell from a third-floor storage compartment, bouncing off another compartment on his way down and, flailing to halt his fall, ripping large strips of skin off both arms. I daresay the process of sifting those pathetic belongings of his—the mad clothing, old magazines, dead letters, hospital supplies, crates of dusty audiotapes and whatnot—had been a melancholy business, and doubtless he'd gotten plastered in the process. Hence the fall.

In Oklahoma City, bandaged like a mummy, he took a room at a motel in a seedy patch of neighborhood off Classen Circle: 19 DOLLARS A DAY, said the sign outside. WEEKLY RATES AVAILABLE. Our dear old high school was visible in the distance, like Gray's Eton where ignorance is bliss. Here he spent almost ten thousand dollars in less than a month. His girlfriend Maryam called my mother and blubbered in that nebulous accent of hers, "He is smoking the *crack* all the time! He is trying to get *me* to smoke the crack!" Scott had apparently managed to segregate his crack-and-hustling life from his church-and-Maryam life over the years, but now the two blurred, and it must have been disconcerting for all concerned. At the motel Maryam found Scott with all sorts of derelict characters; Scott showed up for Sunday services at the Crossroads in a state of nattering lunacy. When, however, my mother arranged to meet Scott for lunch, she stopped by his motel room and saw nothing amiss but a few chaste beers on ice in the bathroom sink. Scott looked a bit gray in the face, a bit banged up, but otherwise seemed in decent fettle.

"Oh, that goddamn Maryam," she told me afterward. "Scott's fine! Well, not *fine*, but I've seen him worse."

A week or so later Scott called her to say he was broke, utterly broke. "I don't know," he said over and over, in the same woebegone way he'd told my father, twenty-five years before, that he'd dropped out of NYU after less than a single semester. "I don't know, Ma." He wanted to live with her again. Turn over a new leaf. When she refused, he sighed but offered little argument; in that case, he said, he wanted to come over and pick up his stereo, his last valuable possession, which he'd left behind that day the cops had removed him from the premises. Marlies forbade him to come anywhere near her house, but arranged for her ex-boyfriend Dave to bring it to Scott's motel.

"What did he look like?" I asked Dave a few months later.

Dave groped for words. He'd always been fond of Scott and vice versa. Finally he just shook his head and said, "I left there feeling very fortunate."

Scott had decided to become a preacher. For those who wonder where preachers come from, it might be interesting to know that there are actually training camps where one spends a month or so studying the Bible, practicing declamatory gestures, and perhaps learning a few financial rudiments—or so I imagine. Whatever the case, one emerges with a diploma, an official man of the cloth, all for a fee of five hundred dollars. Such anyway was the camp Scott planned to attend—and so far so good: he got almost eight hundred dollars for his elaborate stereo system and called our mother in a jubilant mood. He'd report to camp on Friday, he said, and within a month he'd be a bona fide fisher of men. Already he deplored the sinner he'd been in days gone by, to say nothing of his atheist mother and his whole atheist family—bound for the pit.

By Friday his money was gone. "I don't know, I don't know," he told Maryam, begging her to buy him a bottle of gin and take him to a movie, any movie, anything to get outside of himself. She did as he asked; it would have been cruel to refuse; besides, she loved him. In the movie theater Scott drank the whole bottle of gin and commenced a kind of weepy muttering, so that people around him changed their seats or left the show altogether. A total stranger could see that Scott was drowning, drowned.

On Saturday, a day late, Maryam dropped him off at preacher camp. She'd decided to loan him the five hundred dollars; she prayed God would intervene and make Scott a preacher after all—then, perhaps, they could be married. On Monday he was either asked to leave or took it upon himself to abscond with Maryam's money. Anyway, he disappeared for a bit.

I got the news from Marlies, who blustered against that *worthless miserable sonofabitch* and vowed never to trust him again. A few days later Burck called: "Any news of your brother?" he asked, with the usual wincing hesitation, and I told him the whole story—the preacher camp, the hocked stereo, the gin bottle, on and on. I told it for laughs, but my father didn't laugh: Scott had yet to become a remote figure of fun in his eyes. When I mentioned the part about the moviegoers recoiling from poor old boozy Scott, my father seemed to stifle a gasp, as if he'd been knifed.

Scott resurfaced on Valentine's Day, when he gave our mother a call. The moment she heard his voice she let loose a typhoon of abuse, until finally, her anathemas exhausted, she waited for the usual ingenious rebuttal. But there was none. Silence.

"... Scott? You there?"

He breathed. He was there.

At last she said, "Well, anyway, it's Valentine's Day. C'mon, I'll take you to lunch."

They met on a street corner near a place where my mother liked to get dim sum. It wasn't a particularly cold day, but Scott was homeless again and wearing what remained of his wardrobe in layers. This created an impression of bulk. Once they sat in a booth, though, my mother got a good look at her son, or what was left of him—the bony face that even she could no longer wish back to health. Its sallowness bespoke a failing liver, and the eyes leaked weary tears, one after the other, catching in a grayish beard and plopping wearily, at length, onto his plate. One after the other. Scott pushed his food around and wept.

For once my mother was at a loss. "Scott," she said, "you need *help*."

He nodded, then buried his face in a napkin and tried to pull himself together. He let out a shuddery sigh—*shew-ew-ew*—blew his nose into the napkin, and said, hardly a whisper, "I know, Ma."

She offered to take him to a hospital, but he only shook his head. After a dull pause, again and again, she'd repeat some variation of the remark "You need *help*" and Scott would wispily agree. The upshot of the lunch was that she found him an apartment and paid the first month's rent.

That afternoon she called me.

"He needs money!" she said. "He needs to eat! He's dying! He can't pay the heating bill!"

On and on. I listened, amazed. "Where will this end?" I asked her.

"I don't *know*! We can't just let him *die*!"

But I detected, or thought I detected, a very faint inquisitive turn at the end of that statement—as in: "or can we?"—as though she were seeking permission or at least canvassing my viewpoint.

"Let him go," I told her. "Let him go, Mom."

But she couldn't. "I can't! Call your father!"

"Why?"

"I don't know what to do!"

And she burst into tears. So I called my father and explained this latest development. As he got older my father very rarely lost his temper, but a catharsis was long overdue where Scott was concerned.

"He's forty-two years old! Tell him to walk off a tall building!"

I agreed, but pointed out that I lacked the moral authority or whatever to make my mother see it that way. Would he try? Burck sighed, calmed down: he would try. What was left of his love for my mother was little more than a rueful pang, but the very idea of this idle sickly wretch—his *son*—glomming onto an old woman was disgusting. It was disgusting.

SCOTT MUST HAVE agreed, since he dropped out of sight again. He also seemed to agree with the whole tall-building motif. Around this time he took an elevator to the top of Fifty Penn Place—a sentimental journey of sorts, as this was the building where he used to dangle from the horizontal flagpole—only to find the rooftop door was locked nowadays, possibly because of his own antics twenty years before. I heard about this later from Scott's friend Thomas, the musician/waiter, who'd since moved away from the city (leaving Scott all the more desolate). One day Scott had called Thomas and mentioned the fact that he was trying to kill himself but being thwarted by stupid shit like locked doors.

"Fifty Penn Place isn't the only tall building in Oklahoma City," Thomas pointed out.

"Yeah, but it's the only one *nearby*," said Scott. "I'd have to take a bus downtown, you know? Pay a buck. Fuck that."

Surely such acedia was a matter of comic hyperbole. Thomas laughed. Scott laughed. It was a fun conversation. At one point Scott said something like "I'm a double felon and my fucking back hurts all the time. I look like shit. I'm totally unemployable. Nobody wants to see me anymore. What would you do if you were me, Thomas?"

"Talk about a rhetorical question!" his friend laughed. Then he hastened to add that he was *joking*, of course, and urged Scott to seek help at the VA.

Scott did not seek help, until one night he was arrested again. My mother called the station and learned he was charged with breaking and entering; also he'd spat on the arresting officers and gotten a good beating in the bargain.

SCOTT WENT OUT with a certain bravado. The chastened ghost who'd pushed bits of dim sum around his plate on Valentine's Day was, during the last weeks of his life, nowhere in evidence. As always my mother kept tabs on him at the county jail—a ghastly place—where he was, by all accounts, a real live wire: he talked back to guards and prisoners alike, was roundly pummeled, and finally was placed in solitary for his own safety.

To the end my mother believed that if only Scott could stop drinking and drugging, he'd become a productive citizen. She always made a point of saying so when she spoke to him on the phone.

"There's nothing wrong with *me*," Scott would reply, and one night he told her to go fetch a pen. Sulkily he began dictating a suicide note. The tender bits were all for Maryam; what he had to say to us, Burck and me, was loving but defiant: "I miss your pagan asses."

"So I'm going to hell," I said, when my mother told me as much. "Does this mean he's finally going to kill himself, or what?"

My mother deplored my flippancy—"*Nuh!*"—adding that the note had actually been dictated a week or so earlier and Scott was still alive as far as she knew. So perhaps he'd changed his mind.

He hadn't changed his mind. In fact he was waiting for an apt occasion—Good Friday, as it happened, though I'm not sure whether Scott identified more with the martyred Christ or the "good thief" Dismas ("today shalt thou be with me in Paradise"). In any case, just before midnight, he made a slipknot out of his sheets and strangled himself in bed. Efforts to revive him were unavailing.

MARLIES LIKES TO tell of how she got the news that night, as it appeals to her love of both the macabre and the scatological. She'd just woken up with terrible stomach cramps when the phone rang. She knew it was bad news; she knew it had something to do with Scott; but such was the urgency of her condition that she had to grab the cordless with one hand, staggering, and fumble at her panties with the other. She'd just exploded on the toilet when the chaplain said, "I'm afraid I have bad news, Mrs.—"

"And I think he must have *heard* something," said my mother, "since he sort of hesitated, you know? Then he asked me to pray with him. He asked me to get down on my knees. So I said 'Okay, go ahead,' and the whole time I was straining at stool."

Then she bursts out cackling, beet red in the face, subsiding at last with a pensive sigh. "Ah God," she says, dabbing an eye. "Poor Scott."

I didn't get the news until the next afternoon—this from my kindly aunt Kay. The phone rang, and I let the machine get it. "I was just calling to say how sorry I am about Scott," she said, and I picked up the receiver.

"What about Scott?" I asked, though I knew then and there he was dead.

"You haven't heard?"

"No."

"Oh. Well. I'm terribly sorry, sweetie. He, well, he killed himself last night."

"He did? How?"

She told me. At the time everyone thought he'd hanged himself; it was only later, after my mother had gotten the autopsy report, that we learned the actual details. But at the moment I pictured Scott dangling in his cell (when in fact he'd been recumbent), and while the image had pathos, I wasn't quite moved to tears by it. My tenderhearted aunt, though, had begun to sniffle—she hadn't expected to be the one to break the news—and by pausing a lot and sort of groping for words, I was able to convey a semblance of devastation.

After that I called my mother. At the moment she was sitting on the porch with Burck; Sandra had brought him over and left the two alone so they could commiserate about their dead son. Burck sounded composed in a sort of gloomy, irascible way. On the one hand, I think, he wanted to succumb to a seemly grief, while at the same time he was damned if he'd embarrass himself over someone like Scott. I felt rather the same way—if less so—and our talk was awkward and brief.

My wife wouldn't be home for a few hours, and I didn't see any reason to spoil the rest of her day. I went about my afternoon as usual. I took the dog for a walk and tried to think about Scott, but I could only conceive of his suffering in the abstract: he must have felt ill, of course, smothered in aches and pains, and utterly alone in the world (except for Jesus and Maryam); meanwhile his depression would have been worsened by withdrawal from drugs and alcohol. It must have been pretty awful, I thought, but that's about as far as I got.

Later I sat in my study looking through an old photo album. There we were as children, Scott a bit more handsome than I and well aware of it. Again I noticed the complacence with which he regards me in these photos, as though he'd pegged me as a good enough egg but not really to his taste, and certainly not a threat. And I, sitting there at my desk, viewed the comely juvenile Scott with like detachment; the sad part was that I didn't remember him very well. He'd been eclipsed by the later version.

I was still sitting there when Mary came in to kiss me, and by way of explaining the photo album I said, "My brother hanged himself in jail last night." I'd always been dismissive of the whole subject, and I'd meant to make this a rather casual, even callous announcement. But instead I began sobbing and couldn't stop—as if my wife's decency had infected me and suddenly I felt the force of Scott's suffering in this world. Or maybe it was just hearing myself say those terrible words.

The rest of the night I lay on a couch sniffling and sipping gin. I was aware of my wife in the other room, hearing me sniffle and feeling sorry for me, which made me feel all the more sorry for myself but a little disgusted too. It occurred to me that I was thinking more about how sad I seemed than about Scott, who at his best would have laughed at that, or maybe not.

———

SCOTT WAS CREMATED, and a couple of months later my mother held a funeral of sorts in the pet cemetery behind her house. We had discussed, the night before, how things should proceed. My mother wanted me to read Prospero's speech from *The Tempest* ("Our revels now are ended"), but I thought it a hackneyed idea and even in doubtful taste, given the debased nature of Scott's revels. Instead I wanted to read Rupert Brooke's "Clouds," which was elegiac without relating to anything too specific Scottwise. I read it aloud, and Marlies let it pass. She insisted I also read I Corinthians 13, since Scott himself had requested that passage for his obsequies, the better to chide us from beyond the grave for lacking *charity*—which, as St. Paul would have it, "beareth all things, believeth all things, hopeth all things, endureth all things."

"Oh, I get it," I said. "We didn't 'endureth' every bit of his bullshit so now he's *dead*, is that it?"

"This is Scott's funeral," said my mother. "I think his voice should be heard."

So finally I agreed to read it, as long as I got to keep my Rupert Brooke poem. That night my mother also showed me the various funeral accoutrements: the wooden urn that Dave had lovingly carved and polished, Scott's ashes inside (a lot of gravelly bone meal for the most part); the airbrushed portrait of Scott as a sternly handsome marine ("If only he'd stayed in the marines!" my mother sighed); the little pawpaw tree that would be planted at Scott's grave and fertilized with his ashes. Marlies had gotten as many as fifty cards and e-mails from old family friends who'd known and loved Scott as a child. They'd heard his life was troubled, of course, but it's a strange leap from the fussy, precocious little man Scott had been, once upon a time, to the weary bearded lunatic who'd killed himself in jail. When you look at it that way—the one and then the other—life seems a terrible thing.

The funeral was a nice occasion. One of Scott's childhood friends, Kent, was summoned from the ether of almost three decades to give a eulogy. He was meant to represent a more innocent time in Scott's life—also, my mother liked to point out that any number of Scott's old friends had found him *wonderful*, essentially wonderful, whatever his vagaries and chronic bad luck. My rebuttal to this part of her vast apologia on the subject of Scott was that such old friends—Todd the Tortoise, Maryam, Thomas, various church people my mother had met—were every bit as fucked-up as he, albeit some more subtly than others. Kent, then, was Marlies's way of settling my hash on that point: after an admittedly misspent youth—much of it spent with Scott—Kent had gone on to become a successful chef, indeed had moved back to Oklahoma City recently to open his own restaurant; and though he'd been out of touch with Scott for many years, he continued to think of him fondly.

If the world were a stage and Scott's life a play, the dramatis personae would be a large and various menagerie—but in the end there was only a single boyhood chum and family, the least exasperated of whom (my wife) had never met Scott. My uncle Richard had come all the way from Germany, where he'd last seen Scott as a slaphappy drunkard of eighteen. In his baritone broken English, Richard told me that he'd had to knock Scott on his ass a few times, but clearly he'd never given up hope that he and Scott would be reunited in this life amid a lot of beer and laughter. One of the most poignant sights that day was Richard with his loud painted necktie, dashing away tears like a disappointed child and frowning with furious dignity. Also present were my aunt Kay and her husband, a retired army colonel, both of them kindly people who had tried to keep in touch with Scott, at long distance, almost to the end. The whole thing bewildered them. They'd never known Scott to be vicious or stoned or mendacious: as a child he'd been delightful, and as an adult he'd been little more than a diffident voice on the telephone or a card that came twice a year. My father, meanwhile, arrived inscrutably cheerful; Sandra wore a chic mourning outfit, the main flourish of which was a wide beribboned black hat. While we all stood around sipping wine ("since Scott was such a tippler," my mother reminded us), Dave walked back and forth, yeomanlike, setting up the gravesite: the urn, the portrait, the pawpaw tree.

At last we settled in our little semicircle of chairs, in the twinkling leaf-scattered sunlight of a late June morning, and listened to Kent's eulogy. He got off to a bad start, piously proclaiming that if anyone felt any guilt or "negativity" over Scott's death, he or she "should just let it go." My father's vague amiable smile hardened a little. But Kent rallied. Basically he'd brainstormed every good thing he could remember about Scott, typed it all up, and haphazardly rattled off the high points. He nicely elided every hint of the sordid, and even managed to be touching there at the end.

"Whatever Scott did or didn't do," he said, folding his notes with trembling fingers and cramming them into his pocket forever, "I want you to know he loved you all. He always talked about how proud he was of his family."

I doubted whether Kent had known the later Scott well enough to say he "always" talked about one thing or the other—but alas, it was a fair assumption that Scott's love for us had, in fact, never quite failed. He possessed, at bottom, a loving heart.

Next were my readings from Corinthians and Rupert Brooke, and I was determined to be every bit as unflappable as my father, who smiled at me with blank amiability as I stood next to that portrait of Lance Corporal Bailey. All but winking, I informed our fellow mourners that my first reading had been chosen by Scott himself—and I daresay that, yes, we could hear his voice in the charge that one was "nothing" without charity. So that was done. Before I read "Clouds," I explained that Brooke had meant to evoke the perspective of the trenches—*clouds*, to wit: the last thing of nature a soldier in the Great War was likely to see. Then I began to read. At the following lines, though, my voice cracked and crumbled:

> *They say that the Dead die not, but remain*
> *Near to the rich heirs of their grief and mirth.*
> *I think they ride the calm mid-heaven, as these,*
> *In wise, majestic, melancholy train,*
> *And watch the moon, and the still-raging seas,*
> *And men . . .*

It was hard to go on. At the moment it seemed rather likely that Scott would spend eternity in some cloudy limbo, watching us all, the way he used to skulk around strange houses in the middle of the night and stare at family photos on the wall and wish . . . God knows what. I gave my father a helpless look, but his smile had faded like an old poster on a ruined wall. Finally I managed to gasp

> *. . . coming and going on the earth.*

and returned red-faced to my chair. My wife rubbed my back, and Sandra, touched, came over and gave me a hug that made her hat fall off.

Finally we each scooped a bit of Scott's ashes into the hole

Dave had dug for the pawpaw tree. It was planted next to a little plaque that gave Scott's name and the legend:

United States Marine Corps
Born 1960
Died 2003

Next to Scott was the grave of Rosebud, his favorite cat. Rosebud alone had never let on that she minded his incessant, boozy stroking.

My father slipped away as the rest of us headed back to the house, and nobody went looking for him. Maybe twenty minutes later he returned for the feast my mother had prepared with Kent's help. Smiling again, he took his place at the table and began eating with good appetite, as did we all.

FOR A FEW months after his death I thought a lot about Scott, and sometimes I'd cry a little as I remembered reading those lines from Rupert Brooke. Part of me knew such sentiment was maudlin and all for myself—the bereft little brother who could have tried harder—and I'd take a deep breath and think of other things. A better kind of mourning was the times I'd laugh at something and realize that Scott, and perhaps Scott alone, would have laughed too.

It strikes me as odd that I never once dreamed about Scott after his death. Marlies reports the same phenomenon, and it's a lot weirder in her case. She tells me that every other day or so she visits her pet cemetery and sits on the bench next to Scott's pawpaw tree, chattering at him. Whimsically she invests him with the supernatural powers of the dead: "You were a pain in the ass when you were alive, Scott," she notes fondly, "so tomorrow I want you to give us a little rain. My herbs are dying!" Mostly, though, she scolds him for his conspicuous absence from her dreams: "Why don't you ever *visit*?"

"Does he ever answer?" I asked her one day.

"No," she said. She sipped her martini and stared at a hummingbird droning at a feeder there on her porch. "I think he's in a place where he just doesn't think of us anymore."

And I remembered why I'd started crying as a child, thirty-odd years ago, in that paneled room at the back of my grandmother's house in Vinita. Scott had just confided about his second family who lived in the other dimension, and then he'd added—without vindictiveness, as if he were simply stating a poignant, intractable fact—that someday he'd disappear into their loving arms forever.

"You won't even *visit*?" I sobbed.

"No," he said, holding my hand. "I'll never come back."

acknowledgments

This was not an easy book to write; indeed, it took about eleven years in all—during which, granted, a couple of hefty biographies intervened. Amid the many stillborn drafts, I would have been hopelessly stymied without the help of Matt Weiland, an editor of genius and one of the nicest guys I know. "Wow," he'd say, in effect, whenever I presented him with the latest draft, "this is *such* an improvement, Blake. Now all you have to do is . . ." And so on, I know not how many times. Thank you, Matt, for the caress of your velvet goad.

This is my first book with Matt's employer, Norton, and so far it's been wonderful. Sam MacLaughlin is a marvel of efficiency and tact; India Cooper is quite simply the best copy editor I've ever had (and I've been very fortunate in that respect). I also thank the many nice people who have responded so competently via Matt or Sam on points of design, marketing, and whatever else. I look forward to knowing each and every one of you by name.

My thanks to David McCormick, whose services as an agent include being a superlative reader. A very busy man, he spent hours marking up these pages in their various forms, and meanwhile said nothing about the more lucrative work we might have been doing.

My friend Michael Ruhlman was generous, as always, in his enthusiasm for this book, and it's made all the difference. I'm a better writer and human being for knowing him, as I've said before and will certainly have occasion to say again.

Claire Dederer wrote me a long and priceless critique simply because she's an exceptionally nice person and so smart she has to do something with the overflow.

Thanks to the dear old friends of my youth, who have remained friends over the years despite the vagaries recorded in this story, and despite (in some cases) their appearing in this story in whatever form. You know who you are, and you know I love you.

My most heartfelt thanks, by far, to my family. At his best, my brother Scott was a very lovable man, and—in case I haven't made this clear enough yet—he and I had a *great* deal in common, both for better and worse. I tend to laugh whenever I remember him nowadays, and that's not a bad compliment. As for my father, Burck, I hope I've captured something of his sweetness and decency, and I wish him nothing but happiness. Above all, I thank my long-suffering mother, Marlies, who disagrees with certain interpretive points in this book, and yet has been unfailingly helpful, loving, and loyal—to me, to everyone, always. She's an heroic figure in my life, and I wouldn't have made it without her.

To my beloved Mary and Amelia: here we are. It's lovely.